ST. PETER REL. ED. CENTER
1110 MONROE STREET
LA PORTE, INDIANA 46350

D1365753

"The choice for your children is clear. Their liturgies can be either (‗‗‗ ‗‗ many times they're deadly. But there's hope. *Stories, Symbols, Songs and Ski.* ‗‗‗ aine Marie Lee and Elaine Wisdom will make your children's liturgies livelier than you can imagine."

William Griffin
Author, *Jesus For Children*

"Lee and Wisdom have thought of everything! This is a treasure-trove of resources, especially for those planning children's liturgies, teaching a lectionary-based religious education program, or teaching in parochial schools. The ideas are creative and practical, the directions are clear, and the projects can be built from easy-to-find materials. The last chapter, a chart of suggested approaches for teaching the themes of the Sunday readings in all three cycles, will be especially helpful. It puts a panoramic view of the whole year at the catechist's fingertips. What a time-saver and valuable tool for planning!"

Carole MacClennan
Author, *Learning by Doing*

"This very creative book will enable even the most un-creative people to provide variety, interest, and involvement in their sessions with children. Although designed for those preparing children's liturgies, it will be equally helpful for those leading children's Liturgy of the Word celebrations and for classroom catechists who want to make scripture themes come alive for their students. The simple graphics are a god-send for those without an artsy-craftsy bone in their bodies. Simple costumes, pipe-cleaner people, and puppets, among other involvement suggestions, suddenly become useful ideas. All who work with children know that the real creativity lies with them, once the leader has enough confidence to launch the project. This book will provide the confidence!

"The chapters on costumes and the final one providing theme and approach suggestions for all Sundays in all three liturgical cycles are in and of themselves worth putting this volume on the resource shelf in every Religious Education Center."

Stacy Schumacher
Co-author, *Celebrating Holidays*

"I have enjoyed reading *Stories, Symbols, Songs and Skits for Lively Children Liturgies* very much. It provides a rich variety of tools for making liturgies come alive for children. Many examples with clear explanations and detailed illustrations are given for each of the approaches presented.

"I especially enjoyed the chapter entitled 'Bringing the Message Home'; it allows the messages received at the Sunday liturgy to become an integral part of everyday life."

Gayle Schreiber
Author, *Prayer Services for Young Children*

"Any parish beginning a children's liturgy on a regular basis will save themselves a lot of work by using this book as a guide. And those parishes that already have children's liturgies will gain new ideas. The book is simple enough for all to follow, yet it has a great variety of creative ideas. Best of all, it offers great hints for involving the children in liturgies from the planning stage to the evaluations. The book lists the Scripture for all the Sundays of the year and suggests themes and possible creative approaches."

Trudy Schommer
Author, *Easiest Gospel Plays Ever*

"No more boring, dull children's liturgies for those who follow the suggestions in this book. Numerous ideas are offered to make these services more lively and participative—hence, more interesting to the adults who direct them and to the children who benefit from them."

Margrit A. Banta
Pastoral Minister and Author

"Kids love Show-and-Tell and so do I! That's why I love this very helpful book. It not only tells you how to put that 'once upon a time' magic into Scripture stories for children; it also shows you how. The clear illustrations could help anyone learn easy ways to make props, puppets, and all those etceteras that turn liturgies for children into a discovering time they will enjoy—and remember."

Bernadette McCarver Snyder
Author, *150 Fun Facts Found in the Bible*

"This book is a wonderful resource not only for children's liturgies, but for classes, retreats—any gathering of children. Examples, instructions, and diagrams are plentiful and easy to follow. I already have several projects in mind for our religious education retreats and classes. I can't wait to share this book with our catechists!"

Karen Leslie
Coordinator of Religious Education
Author, *Faith and Little Children*

How to Use

Stories, Symbols, Songs and Skits

for Lively Children's Liturgies

Anne Marie Lee and Elaine Wisdom

TWENTY-THIRD PUBLICATIONS

Mystic, CT 06355

Acknowledgments

The authors wish to acknowledge and thank the following for their support and encouragement: the R.C.E. community; Breid Ryan, Librarian; and a very patient husband, David Lee.

North American Edition 1995

First published in 1994 by

The Columba Press
93 The Rise
Mount Merrion, Blackrock
Co. Dublin, Ireland

Illustrations by Elaine Wisdom, R.C.E.

Twenty-Third Publications
185 Willow Street
P.O. Box 180
Mystic, CT 06355
(203) 536-2611
800-321-0411

ISBN 0-89622-640-9
Library of Congress Catalog Card Number 94-61925

© Copyright 1995 Anne Marie Lee and Elaine Wisdom, R.C.E.. All rights reserved. No part of this publication may be reproduced in any manner without prior written permission of the publisher. Write to Permissions Editor.

Printed in the U.S.A.

To Kate and Anna
and all the children
who have helped us in the making of this book

CONTENTS

Jesus called the children to him and said,
"Let the little children come to me, and do not stop them;
for it is to such as these that the kingdom of God belongs."
Luke 18:16

INTRODUCTION

Christian liturgy is created when a group of believers gather to share and celebrate their faith. Anything that can help these gatherings to come alive in understanding the scripture and in deepening an appreciation of the Christian mystery is to be welcomed and encouraged. It is in this belief that we offer this book as a resource for anyone involved in helping to create children's liturgy. We have concentrated on visual imaging because it seems to us that much has already been written on the tradition and use of music in liturgy.

Very few people could read in the early days of the church and, because of this, the pre-Reformation church and those of the Eastern rite developed a great historical tradition of imaging the important Christian events through the decoration of their churches. They also used the symbolism and drama of their rites and celebrations as a means of expounding the scriptures and teaching the Christian faith.

Examples of visual imaging as an aid to worship are seen in the use of statues and of paintings, particularly in the traditional sequence known as "The Stations of the Cross," which portrays Christ carrying his cross and the people he met along the way. The use of icons in the Eastern church is also becoming increasingly known and accepted in our Western tradition. Right up to the present day, certain churches have commissioned artists to paint or sculpt their interpretation of key Christian events. Such visual aids help the rest of us connect more concretely with these events and their meaning for our own lives.

The area of visual imaging is rich with possibility and potential. In the field of education there is a growing awareness, acknowledgment, and development in the use of drama and visual stimulation to facilitate the child's learning process. Children love to see things unfold before their eyes. Their attention is held by color and movement. Most exciting of all is when they can take part in the activity themselves.

If you have not yet started a children's liturgy in your church, you may feel hesitant about doing so. There is no need to feel this way. Gather around you others who are interested, always include children, and involve your priest or pastor. Start with simple ideas and, as you grow in confidence, you will become more adventurous. Always listen carefully to the children. They are the best creators of their liturgy.

Children have wonderful imaginations and the simplest props will take them into the story. Some of you will be lucky enough to have artistic talent among your group, but don't be put off if you haven't. If you cannot draw or paint free-hand, you can trace, enlarge, cut out, color, or make collages from old magazines, or odds and ends of material. It is amazing what inventiveness is found in the most inexperienced groups where children and enthusiasm are among the motivators.

There is a great sense of joy and satisfaction in working with children in this way, especially when they are able to tell you afterwards what the celebration was all about. In that case, you have done a good job! Take notes and keep the ideas for next year.

This book includes only the ideas born out of our experience. We hope what you find in it will stimulate you into coming up with your own ideas for presenting the rich themes of scripture and belief in whatever way suits the needs of your particular church group best. We have left space at the end of each chapter for you to make your own notes.

May God bless you in the work of bringing his Word to children, and we hope you will know great satisfaction and deep joy as a result of your efforts.

CHAPTER 1

APPROACHES TO PRESENTING THE WORD

STORYTELLING

A well-told story is a pleasure to listen to, both for children and adults. The gospel stories are rich in content and have a wide scope for scene setting and modernizing.

The storyteller should know the story well and hold eye contact with the children while telling it. Inviting the children to comment or answer questions throughout the story helps to hold their attention. Encourage the children to interact with the biblical characters. You, the storyteller, might dress up for the part. However, if you do, be ready for some "smart" children to point out that glasses and watches weren't invented yet!

People, including children, are always interested in the mundane events of other people's daily lives—what they wore, the food they ate, their work or games, their arguments, and their laughter. Bible stories can be fleshed out with such details. Take, for example, the story of Jonah trying to escape from God (Jon 1:1–16).

> In this story God tells Jonah to go to the city of Nineveh and speak out against it. Jonah doesn't want to go, so he goes off in the other direction on a journey that includes a ride on a ship to Spain. During this journey, there is a dangerous storm and the sailors are very frightened and pray to their gods for help. They throw off some of the cargo into the sea to lessen the danger. The sailors wake Jonah up and ask him who he is and who his god is. They draw lots to see who might have angered the gods and started this storm. Jonah draws the short straw and he admits that he is the cause of the storm because he is running away from God. He advises the sailors to throw him into the sea

> and the storm will abate. Reluctantly they do this, and the storm ceases. The sailors are then in fear and awe of Jonah's God and they vow to offer sacrifices to him and to serve him.

This is a very rich story. The storyteller could dress as the ship's captain and tell a little about life as a sailor in those days. Describe the ship and the food and clothing of the sailors. What did they use for light at night and how did they cook? Tell the children a little bit about the gods the sailors worshiped, and that they were quite superstitious. A map from that time period could be reproduced on acetate and, with the use of the overhead projector, you could show the children the distance between Joppa and Spain. As the story is told, it could be illustrated with some drawings, or the use of mime and props, such as a large cardboard box converted to a ship.

Or take the story of God calling Samuel (1 Sm 3:1–21):

> This is the story about God calling Samuel when Samuel was a young boy living with his teacher Eli, who was, at this time, almost blind. They had both gone to bed: Eli in his room, while Samuel slept in the sanctuary of the temple. God called Samuel, who got up and went to Eli, thinking it was he who had called. This happened three times and on the third time Eli realized God was calling Samuel and he told the boy how to respond when it happened again.

This is a lovely story which has great appeal to children. Tell them a little about why young boys were handed over by their parents to the Temple to be trained to serve God. This practice has lasted in different religions even up to the present day. Two children could mime the event as the story is told. What subjects did children like Samuel learn, could they read and write, or were they dependent on the oral tradition? Samuel's mother, Hannah, had given him to the priest, Eli, because she had longed for a son and had promised God that, if she did have a son, she would give him up to serve God in the Temple.

MIME

Mime is the acting out of a scene without dialogue. The mime may tell its own story or a narrator might read a story while the actors perform it. Mime enhances the message of a story and helps the audience to remember it more clearly. Mime has advantages over drama in a church or hall where the acoustics or sound system are not effective. It gives opportunity for a wider group of children to participate and allows young children, who cannot read or memorize lines, to take part as well.

THE HISTORY OF MIME

In the Middle Ages, a religious rite or ceremony could be called a *mystery*, hence the name *Mystery play* for the dramatization of a religious theme. Mime was the forerunner of drama, but both were used extensively in the Middle Ages by the church to bring the faith to the people. Mystery plays were written in Latin by priests who also acted in them, along with members of trade guilds or unions. The guilds and union members took on the parts relevant to their line of work: The goldsmith guild members would have played the three wise kings; a carpenters' guild member might have played the part of Joseph, and so on. This tradition, begun in the Middle Ages, is still carried on in parts of England to this day, for example, the Mystery play held at York. In the German village of Oberammergau, a Passion play has been performed by the villagers every ten years since 1634. Passion plays are also performed in the United States.

EXAMPLE

The following mime was performed at a children's liturgy:

Theme: "Workers in the Vineyard" (Mt 20: 1–16).

Props: A bale of hay was in front of the altar with five garden rakes leaning against it. On the back wall above the altar was a banner which read "Jesus Is Challenging Our Values." To the right of the altar was a tall stand with a large orange circle on top, representing sunrise to sunset.

Characters: The characters were the vineyard owner, his manager, and about twelve idle laborers, all dressed in the costume of the day. The laborers were sitting or standing chatting. The celebrant of the Mass read the gospel story slowly, and the actors played out the scene. The owner came to the idle workers during the day and bargained with them over wages. The laborers took up rakes and began to work. The manager wrote the deals down in his scroll until, at the end of the day, the owner paid out the agreed wages. When the workers compared their wages, they began to argue with the owner and to complain among themselves.

The whole performance was very well played and well received by the congregation. Now, you may ask, "What were they doing with a bale of hay and garden rakes?" Well, not everyone lives near vineyards, so the actors were setting a scene of country life and outdoor work that their congregation would be familiar with. It worked!

In Devon, England, a Nativity play was performed at Christmas by the children of the village school in the local Anglican church. There were soldiers, shepherds, angels, wise men, innkeepers, Mary, Joseph, and the child. The mime was performed while the children sang appropriate carols illustrating the sequence of events. While the small soldiers, shepherds, etc., marched around the church searching for the baby Jesus, one child climbed the steps of the pulpit and held up a star for the wise men to see.

Every child in the school had a part to play in the performance and parents and teachers were occupied for hours beforehand, rehearsing them and preparing costumes and props.

TIPS

When performing a mime or drama, you can add extra characters as long as they don't alter the meaning of the piece of scripture. For example, in the story of the wise and foolish virgins, you could add a shopkeeper, his assistant, and a few customers in the shop where the oil is sold. In the story of the ten lepers, you could add some officials who banish them from public areas, some onlookers, and maybe a physician who examines them and declares them to be lepers. By adding extra characters, you are allowing more children to take part. Also the addition of a little appropriate humor will be much appreciated.

DRAMA

A drama tells a story by means of action and speech. Simple drama has been performed since ancient times, notably in Greek culture, where it is thought to have been derived from religious ceremonies.

Drama is useful in children's liturgies when the children are old enough to read, learn lines, and remember them for the performance.

The public address system must be adequate and the children must be taught how to use it to the greatest advantage. Mime is the best medium where the public address system is inadequate.

The drama should be short, simple, to the point, and relevant to the theme of the day. The children can be dressed up for their parts or not, depending on the story line. For example, in a drama depicting bullying on the school playground, the children would not need to dress up. For a parable from the New Testament, the children could wear costumes from that time.

In order to enhance the sacredness and dignity of the occasion, it is essential in drama and mime to have a practice time before each celebration. However, it is not necessary to attain perfection. Small mistakes and bouts of nervousness are well tolerated by the congregation at a family or children's service.

We suggest you write your own simple scripts. Children are full of ideas and will probably write their own scripts with encouragement from you. Bring together a small group of children to work with at a time. Allow the children to use their own language, for example, a group of our children wrote a Nativity play and some of the script went as follows:

Mary and Joseph are going to Bethlehem. Mary rides on a donkey consisting of two children. The one in front wears a cardboard donkey's head, and a brown blanket is thrown over the backs of both children. Mary leans against the donkey as though riding it, but she is actually walking.

Joseph: Move along donkey, you're so slow.
Donkey: I have a terrible pain in my back. Mary is so heavy.
Joseph: Aw, come on, we're nearly there.
Donkey: No, I'm not budging.
Mary: Joseph, maybe we should have a little rest? We're all quite tired. . . .

Because the donkey wasn't expected to speak, this section was quite lighthearted. Yet, it gave a sense of the length and hardship of the journey. There is no harm in allowing a gentle sense of humor to prevail.

In the script, when Mary went to visit Elizabeth, the same group of children had Elizabeth dress with a pillow under the front of her robe to simulate pregnancy. When Elizabeth rushed out to greet Mary she stopped suddenly, held her abdomen and said, "Oops, a kick," and then went on with the greeting. "For as soon as I heard your greeting, the baby within me jumped with gladness" (Lk 1: 44).

If the children are writing their own scripts for drama, there will be no problem with culture or dialect because they will write as they speak. Both they and their audience will feel comfortable with the end product.

NOTES ON STORYTELLING/MIME/DRAMA:

CHAPTER 2

MAKING THE COSTUMES

Most playschools and many homes have a dress-up box, where children will spend hours in the world of their imagination, dressing themselves up as characters from history, science fiction, television, and story books. Dressing up as characters from the bible is fun, the materials are easy to come by, and the costumes are simple to make. It also allows many children to participate, particularly where there is a crowd scene.

In biblical times, there were rich people, poor people, carpenters, merchants, soldiers, priests, princesses, kings, queens, shepherds, rabbis, fishermen, farmers, children, angels, and prophets.

TYPES OF CLOTHING

The fabric from which the people made their clothes was homespun and, depending on their wealth, could be made from wool, cotton, linen, or silk. The material was dyed with natural dyes made from plants and animals. The fixative used with some dies is called a *mordant* and comes from certain shellfish. So many shellfish had to be crushed for the smallest amount of purple dye, that only the wealthy could afford it. Purple, therefore, was the color worn by emperors, kings, and priests. "There was a rich man who used to dress in purple and fine linen and feast magnificently every day" (Lk 16:19). Purple is also the color of vestment worn by the priest at a Mass during Lent in the Roman Catholic Church.

Color, then, played an important part in biblical times, as it still does in the liturgical year of today and our lives in general.

Animal skins were used for clothing and for carrying water and wine. Skins were also tanned to make leather for sandals, belts, bags, and armor. Parchment, on which the scribes wrote, could also be made from animal skins. You can make paper look like parchment by holding the edge a couple of inches above a flame and browning it. (Only adults should try this!)

In Jesus' day, just as today, you could often tell the race, religion, or profession of a person by the way they were dressed.

COSTUMES

Materials:
• old plain or striped cotton or lightweight skirts;
• towels, large and small;
• old sheets;
• dressing gowns;
• old curtain material, netting and lining;
• men's shirts;
• T-shirts;
• safety pins;
• neck and head scarves;
• strips of material for belts and headbands;
• costume jewelry—bangles, colored beads, etc.;
• old belts.

These materials will provide the range of types of dress that you may require, as illustrated on the following pages. Use your own creativity in adapting these to your particular needs.

An adult's knee-length skirt will be ankle-length on a child. If the waistband of the skirt is worn high under the child's arms, it should be safety-pinned to the T-shirt underneath. If worn at waist level, it can be held on with a waistband and tied at the back. A small towel can be used to make a headdress or a shawl. A large towel may be worn around the waist, as you would after a shower, with a T-shirt for a top. Curtain material may be cut into squares or rectangles to make shawls, cloaks, or loose wraparound garments. Men's shirts, with the sleeves and collars removed, make excellent tunics. Wrap a cloth band or belt around the waist. T-shirts are useful as bases onto which shawls and skirts can be safety-pinned. Dressing gowns serve as the loose coat-like garment of the time, or they can be worn as cloaks.

HEADGEAR

Materials:

- square pieces of lightweight material;
- scissors;
- measuring tape;
- pencil/markers/crayons/paints;

- silver tinsel;
- silver and colored foil;
- cardboard (cereal boxes, etc);
- staples;

- plastic bowl;
- adhesive tape;
- glue;
- safety pins.

These materials can be used in a variety of ways to create a variety of headgear. For example, silver and colored foil can be scrunched up and stapled on to circlets of cardboard to give the impression of precious jewels. The colored foil from candy wrappers is very useful here. Cardboard from cereal boxes can be cut up and used to make headpieces, helmets, halos, and so on. Other simpler headgear can be made from towels, scarves, or rectangular pieces of material, tied on with string or strips of material.

The illustrations on the following pages show simply-made headgear for a variety of different characters.

CIRCLET HEADPIECE

1. CUT OUT A CARDBOARD STRIP ABOUT 2"-4" IN WIDTH AND STAPLE ENDS SECURELY.

2. COVER WITH FOIL.

3. LEAVE PLAIN, OR DECORATE WITH CANDY-WRAPPER JEWELS.

CIRCLET FOR AN EMPRESS

1. MEASURE CHILD'S HEAD.

2. CUT OUT A CARDBOARD STRIP OF THIS LENGTH AND SLOT TOGETHER AT A.

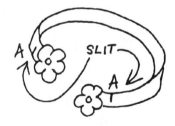

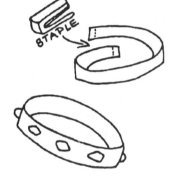

ANGEL'S HALO

1. START WITH A DINNER PLATE-SIZED CIRCLE OF CARDBOARD.

2. CUT INNER HOLE, APPROXIMATELY THE SIZE OF A SMALL PLATE.

3. COVER WITH FOIL.

SOLDIERS' HELMETS

1. CUT OUT THE TWO NARROW SIDES OF A CEREAL B(

2. CUT A FRONT BAND WITH NOSE-GUARD FROM ONE LENGTH.

3. COVER WITH FOIL.

4. STAPLE TOGETHER.

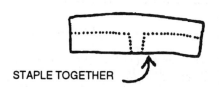

STAPLE TOGETHER

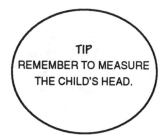

TIP
REMEMBER TO MEASURE
THE CHILD'S HEAD.

STAPLE →  ← STAPLE

AN ADVANTAGE OF THIS HELMET IS THAT IT CAN BE REVERSED TO MAKE A CROWN OR A HEADDRESS.

CROWN

1. LENGTH OF CARDBOARD OF DESIRED DEPTH.

2. CUT OUT AS SHOWN.

CROWN

HEADDRESS

STAPLE ENDS

3. PAINT/COVER WITH FOIL AND DECORATE WITH CANDY-WRAPPER JEWELS.

SHORT TUNIC

(You can adjust the length of the tunic by using different lengths of material.)

1. Use a long rectangle of plain or striped cloth, folded lengthwise in the middle.

2. Mark middle of center fold and cut "V" for the child's head. (It can be enlarged by cutting a slit down the front.)

3. Slip over child's head and tie at the waist. It may need to be stitched a little to prevent too much of a gap at the sides.

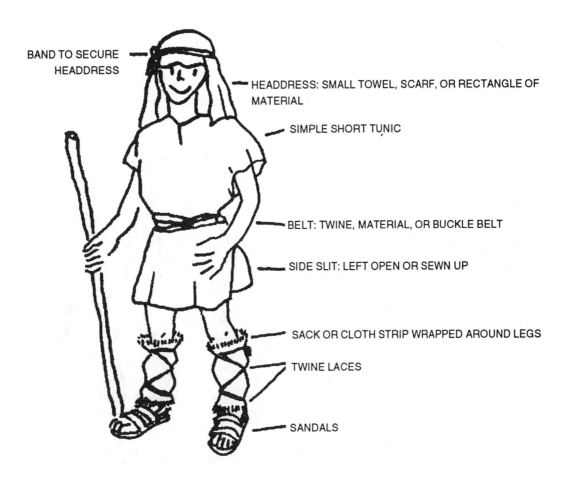

BAND TO SECURE HEADDRESS

HEADDRESS: SMALL TOWEL, SCARF, OR RECTANGLE OF MATERIAL

SIMPLE SHORT TUNIC

BELT: TWINE, MATERIAL, OR BUCKLE BELT

SIDE SLIT: LEFT OPEN OR SEWN UP

SACK OR CLOTH STRIP WRAPPED AROUND LEGS

TWINE LACES

SANDALS

TURBAN

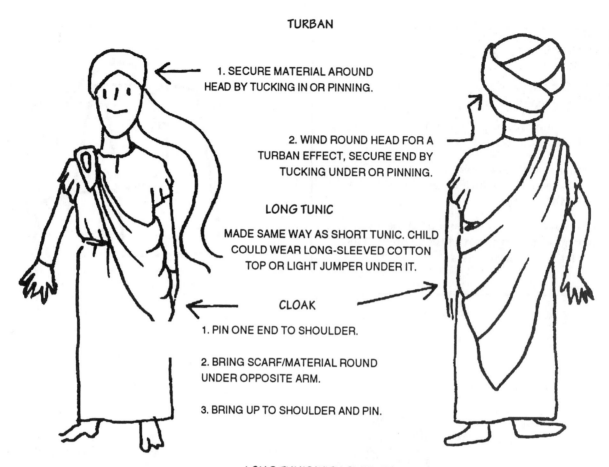

1. SECURE MATERIAL AROUND HEAD BY TUCKING IN OR PINNING.

2. WIND ROUND HEAD FOR A TURBAN EFFECT, SECURE END BY TUCKING UNDER OR PINNING.

LONG TUNIC

MADE SAME WAY AS SHORT TUNIC. CHILD COULD WEAR LONG-SLEEVED COTTON TOP OR LIGHT JUMPER UNDER IT.

CLOAK

1. PIN ONE END TO SHOULDER.

2. BRING SCARF/MATERIAL ROUND UNDER OPPOSITE ARM.

3. BRING UP TO SHOULDER AND PIN.

LONG TUNIC WITH SLEEVES

MEASURE CHILD ACROSS SHOULDERS

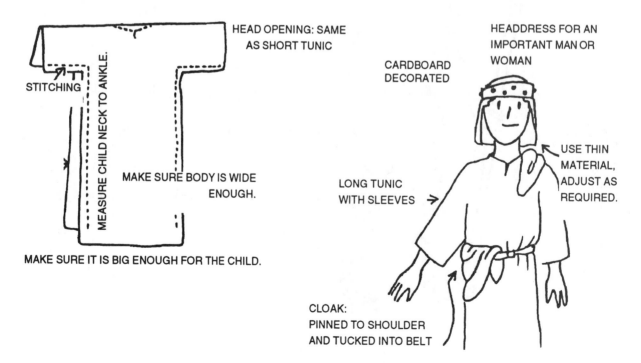

STITCHING

MEASURE CHILD NECK TO ANKLE.

HEAD OPENING: SAME AS SHORT TUNIC

MAKE SURE BODY IS WIDE ENOUGH.

MAKE SURE IT IS BIG ENOUGH FOR THE CHILD.

HEADDRESS FOR AN IMPORTANT MAN OR WOMAN

CARDBOARD DECORATED

LONG TUNIC WITH SLEEVES →

USE THIN MATERIAL, ADJUST AS REQUIRED.

CLOAK:
PINNED TO SHOULDER AND TUCKED INTO BELT

WOMEN'S TUNIC AND VEIL

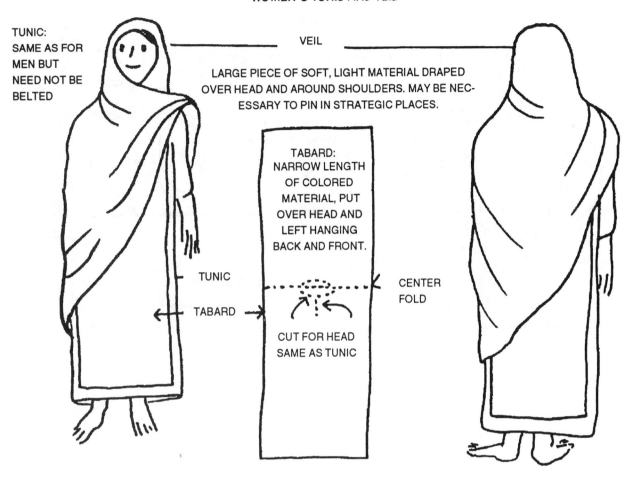

TUNIC:
SAME AS FOR
MEN BUT
NEED NOT BE
BELTED

VEIL

LARGE PIECE OF SOFT, LIGHT MATERIAL DRAPED
OVER HEAD AND AROUND SHOULDERS. MAY BE NEC-
ESSARY TO PIN IN STRATEGIC PLACES.

TABARD:
NARROW LENGTH
OF COLORED
MATERIAL, PUT
OVER HEAD AND
LEFT HANGING
BACK AND FRONT.

TUNIC

TABARD

CENTER
FOLD

CUT FOR HEAD
SAME AS TUNIC

SOLDIERS

ARM GUARD

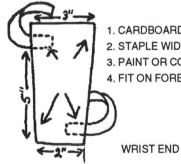

3"

5"

2"

WRIST END

1. CARDBOARD CUT TO SUIT SIZE OF CHILD.
2. STAPLE WIDE ELASTIC TO EACH SIDE TO FIT CHILD.
3. PAINT OR COVER WITH FOIL.
4. FIT ON FOREARM/LEG JUST ABOVE THE WRIST AND BELOW THE KNEE.

SHIN GUARD

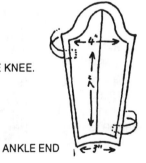

4"

ANKLE END

3"

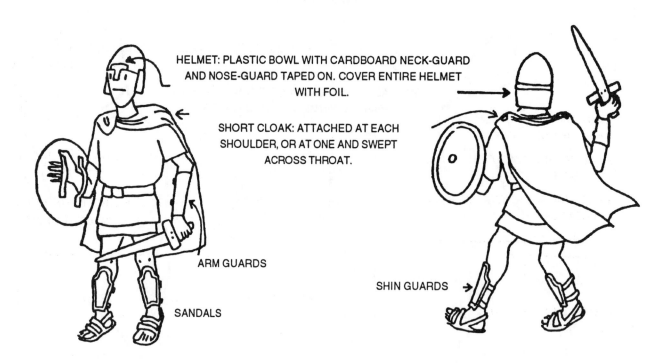

HELMET: PLASTIC BOWL WITH CARDBOARD NECK-GUARD AND NOSE-GUARD TAPED ON. COVER ENTIRE HELMET WITH FOIL.

SHORT CLOAK: ATTACHED AT EACH SHOULDER, OR AT ONE AND SWEPT ACROSS THROAT.

ARM GUARDS

SANDALS

SHIN GUARDS

COSTUME: LARGE T-SHIRT BELTED AT WAIST, WORN OVER MATERIAL WRAPPED AT WAIST AND SECURED.

SHIELD

1. USE A LARGE CIRCLE OF CARDBOARD.

2. STAPLE ON PREPARED CARDBOARD ARM AND HAND GRIPS.

3. COVER WITH FOIL OR PAINT.

(EARLY ROMAN SHIELDS WERE SMALL AND ROUND, MADE OF WOOD AND COVERED WITH HIDE.)

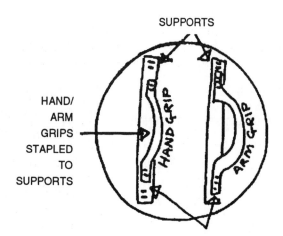

SUPPORTS

HAND/ ARM GRIPS STAPLED TO SUPPORTS

HAND GRIP

ARM GRIP

PREPARED CARDBOARD GRIPS ON SUPPORTS STAPLED TO SHIELD

ANGEL'S WINGS

LEAVE A WING TAB ON EACH
WING TO ATTACH TO CENTER BAR

1. CUT TWO WINGS OUT OF THE BACK AND FRONT OF A CEREAL BOX.

2. USE NARROW SIDE OF BOX OR CUT STRIP 3" X 12" FOR THE CENTER BAR. ATTACH RIBBON.

3. CUT STRIP APPROXIMATELY 3" X 6" TO USE AS A SPREAD BAR.

4. SCORE AND BEND AT DOTTED LINES.

5. STAPLE TO WINGS JUST BELOW TABS FOR CENTER BAR.

6. STAPLE WING TABS TO CENTER BAR AT A SLIGHT ANGLE, ABOUT 4" APART.
7. COVER WITH FOIL.

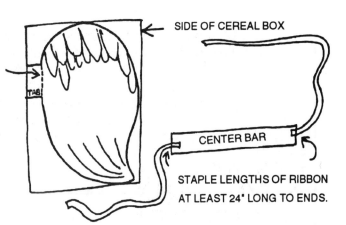

SIDE OF CEREAL BOX

CENTER BAR

STAPLE LENGTHS OF RIBBON AT LEAST 24" LONG TO ENDS.

TIPS

- Leave wing foil plain or draw in feather shapes with black marker.

- Remember to staple spread bar to wings before stapling wings to center bar. If done the other way, it is very difficult to staple the spread bar.

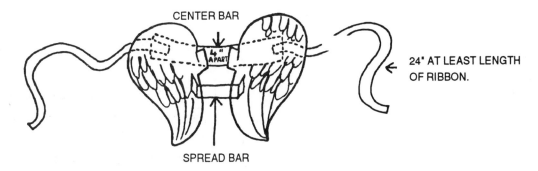

CENTER BAR

24" AT LEAST LENGTH OF RIBBON.

SPREAD BAR

ANGEL'S WINGS II
1. CUT OUT TWO WINGS AS BEFORE.
2. CUT OUT CENTER BAR AS BEFORE AND ATTACH RIBBONS.
3. STAPLE WINGS TO BAR TO LIE FLAT ACROSS THE BACK.

FOOTWEAR

In most cases, the children will wear their own clothes under their costumes. On special occasions, where they want to be fully engaged in their parts, they might go barefoot or wear one of the following: sandals on bare feet, ballet shoes with the ribbon crisscrossed up to the knee, black sneakers with black ribbon crisscrossed up to the knee.

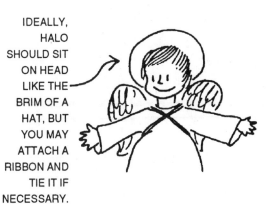

IDEALLY, HALO SHOULD SIT ON HEAD LIKE THE BRIM OF A HAT, BUT YOU MAY ATTACH A RIBBON AND TIE IT IF NECESSARY.

TO ATTACH WINGS: RIBBONS FROM CENTER BAR ARE BROUGHT FROM UNDER CHILD'S ARMS TO FRONT, CROSSED AND TAKEN BACK UP OVER THE SHOULDERS. THEY CAN BE TIED BEHIND THE NECK OR AT THE CENTER BAR.

14

NOTES ON COSTUMES:

CHAPTER 3

MAKING AND USING PROPS

The most effective prop at your disposal will be the imagination of your audience. Use it to its full extent. A few well chosen words before a performance will set the scene in the minds of the congregation.

Elaborate props will not be necessary—existing church furniture can be converted for your use. For example, a table turned on its side makes a screen for the humans behind the hand puppets.

Cardboard boxes, redesigned, covered, or painted, can become chariots, houses, walls, tables, donkey's heads, and boats. Once the children dress up for their parts, the particular scene is set by adding some appropriate implements, for example, a carpenter's workshop comes alive when the children pretend to saw a length of wood placed between two chairs.

A bale of hay, a length of rope, and some garden tools help to create an image of a field or vineyard.

A market setting may be created with upturned boxes covered with cloth and laid with a variety of colorful items for sale, with some children sitting cross-legged at their stalls while potential customers wander around looking and bargaining.

A table or upturned box with a white cloth, a wooden bowl with fruit, a loaf of bread, some cheese, and drinking vessels becomes the setting for a meal, where many scripture stories take place.

A covered table with a scroll placed in the center, and a benediction candelabra or candlestick, gives an atmosphere of Temple or synagogue.

Lanterns for the wise and foolish virgins may be made from folded paper or from empty wine cartons with windows cut in the sides (see diagrams on the following page). Colored cellophane paper pasted to the insides of the windows gives a pleasant glow when a flashlight is placed inside.

A river or lake can be represented by a length of blue cloth placed on the floor, with a child at each end causing it to ripple gently. Garden net can serve as a fishing net and fish can be made by cutting out cardboard shapes. Scripture messages might be written on the fish and the children can catch them out of the river or lake with a stick, line, and hook. The fish should have a cotton or nylon loop taped at the mouth for the hook to catch. The shape of the fish can be adapted as necessary, but the dimensions should be about 8" long by 5"-6" wide.

Another idea would be to hand the fish out to the children and ask them to put their names on them. Then put all the fish in the river and ask the children to fish one out. The children will then be asked to remember in their prayers during the week the child whose name is on the fish they caught.

A foldable wooden frame or screen, about 6' high and 12' wide, made in two sections and hinged together, would be useful to hang backdrops, paintings, and drawings and to use as a screen.

Bundles of dried grass are good for outdoor scenes such as the harvest stories, disciples eating ears of corn on the Sabbath, etc. Ask the children and their families to collect grasses while they are out walking in the summer. Tie them in bundles and hang them upside down in a warm, airy place to dry.

Children are just as sentimental as adults and, if you keep props in storage for next year, the children will delight in recounting their memories when the old props are brought out for use again. They may want them used in exactly the same way as before, just as they like the same story to be told over and over again.

LANTERNS

A SIMPLE PAPER LANTERN

1. TAKE A SHEET OF LARGE PAPER AND FOLD LENGTHWISE.

2. MAKE 2"-3" SLITS ALONG THE FOLDED EDGE.

3. UNFOLD AND BEND THE OTHER WAY TO MAKE A TUBE.

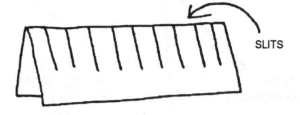

SLITS

4. SLIGHTLY PRESS THE TOP AND BOTTOM TOGETHER TO HELP THE SLITS TO OPEN. IF THEY DO NOT OPEN, YOU MAY NEED TO LENGTHEN THE SLITS.

5. JOIN WITH GLUE OR TAPE.

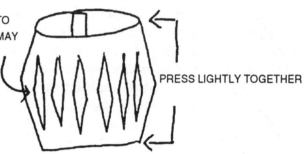

PRESS LIGHTLY TOGETHER

6. CUT A THIN STRIP OF PAPER AND GLUE OR TAPE ON FOR THE HANDLE.

A LANTERN FROM EMPTY WINE CARTON

1. CUT OUT WINDOWS FROM TWO OR FOUR SIDES.

2. FROM THE INSIDE, COVER WITH YELLOW OR RED CELLOPHANE.

3. PAINT OR COVER THE OUTSIDE WITH BLACK PAPER.

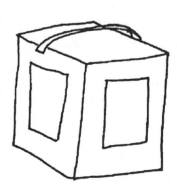

FISH

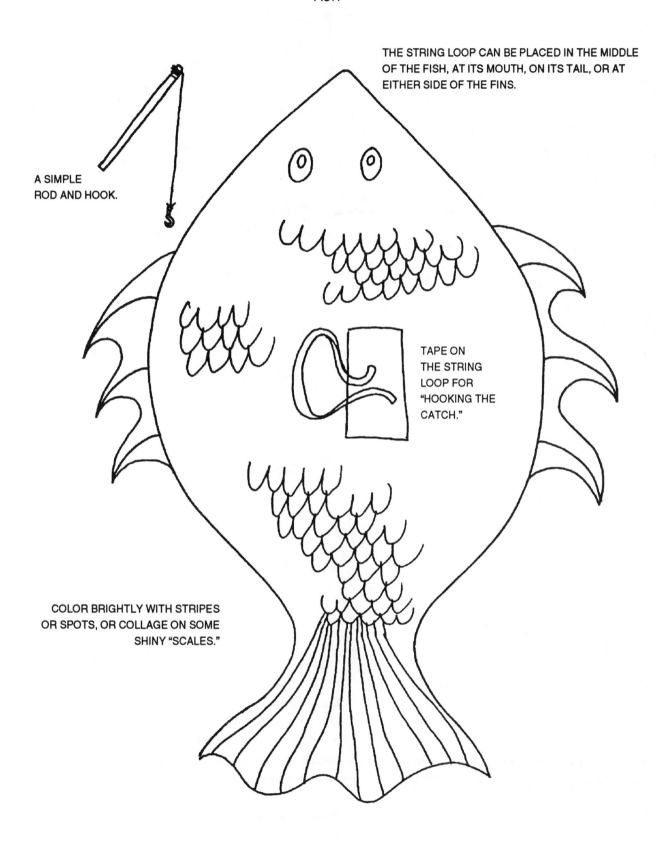

THE STRING LOOP CAN BE PLACED IN THE MIDDLE OF THE FISH, AT ITS MOUTH, ON ITS TAIL, OR AT EITHER SIDE OF THE FINS.

A SIMPLE ROD AND HOOK.

TAPE ON THE STRING LOOP FOR "HOOKING THE CATCH."

COLOR BRIGHTLY WITH STRIPES OR SPOTS, OR COLLAGE ON SOME SHINY "SCALES."

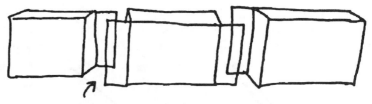

THESE FORM THE CROSS-BAR.

CROSS

A life-sized cross made from large cereal boxes will be very light for a child to carry. You will need the following materials:

- seven same-sized cereal boxes;
- some wide tape;
- a stapler;
- sheets of brown wrapping paper.

Open both ends of the boxes, and place one flap inside the other. Staple the flaps together, close boxes and tape securely end-to-end, cover them with brown paper.

FROM THE MIDDLE BOX, ATTACH ONE BOX ABOVE AND THREE BELOW, USING THE SAME MEANS TO ATTACH THEM.

WHEN COMPLETED AND SECURELY FASTENED, COVER WITH BROWN WRAPPING PAPER.

WITH A DARK FELT PEN, YOU COULD DRAW ON WOODGRAIN MARKING IF YOU WISH.

EASTER GARDEN

A very beautiful Easter garden can be built on a fairly large scale without much difficulty and the children will enjoy bringing in items for it. One or two adults will need to take responsibility for co-ordinating the project, by controlling what comes in and labeling items on loan, in order to ensure that they are returned to the rightful owners.

Choose a suitable place in your church or hall, against a wall or in a corner. Place a waterproof sheet on the floor as a base for the garden and cover it with sand, pebbles, or moss. Build a tomb with a cardboard box covered and lined with gray cloth or plastic to resemble stone. Strong gray or black paper might also be used for the tomb, but it may get damp when the garden is being watered. Decorate the tomb with moss or ivy and the garden with potted plants, flowers, and shrubs. You may be lucky enough to be able to borrow a miniature fountain or waterfall suitable for indoors. If not, use a piece of mirror for a lake or pond.

To this garden can be added a wide variety of butterflies, birds, animals, and people. See Chapter 6, on sculpture, for ideas on making figures for your Easter garden, such as the women who saw where Jesus was laid to rest on Good Friday, the women who went to anoint him on the morning after the Sabbath, the figure of Jesus laid in the tomb covered with a white cloth, and the figure of Jesus whom Mary Magdalene thought was the gardener. Angels, soldiers, and bystanders can also be added, along with a shepherd and some sheep (see diagram in Chapter 10).

THE JESSE TREE

You may wish to have a Jesse tree, celebrating the ancestry of Jesus, during the Advent season. It is usually an evergreen tree with symbols hanging from its branches.

The name *Jesse* comes from Jesse, the father of King David, and as the bible tells us, Jesus is of the line of David. The Jesse tree represents the royal "family tree" of Jesus (Mt 1:1–17), and shows his "roots." The image of the tree is taken from Isaiah 11:1: "A shoot shall sprout from the stump of Jesse, and from his roots a bud shall blossom." The shoot is traditionally regarded as Mary, and the blossom as Jesus.

The tree is also symbolic of the Tree of Life. It began to appear in German art and books in the eleventh century and then appeared throughout Europe in stained glass, sculpture, and manuscripts. The Jesse tree itself is a modern development, designed in 1949 by an American nun. It is a symbol of joyful expectation, the true meaning of Advent. Symbols like the Jesse tree can help us in our reflections while waiting for Christmas. The symbols to be hung on the tree can be made from any material. The most successful we ever made were cut from thin white poster board and drawn on with thick, black-felt pen. The white and black against the green tree was very effective.

The tree is placed in the sanctuary after the 8th of December. Stress that it is not a Christmas tree, so it should not have lights, glitter, or colored balls "decorating" it. Symbols can be placed on the tree each Sunday. For the benefit of the congregation, a sign should also be placed beside the tree, explaining each symbol and giving its scriptural text or reference. Some examples of appropriate symbols are listed below.

THESE SYMBOLS COULD BE PUT ON THE TREE BEFORE CHRISTMAS EVE:

Triangle	Relates to the Godhead of Jesus	**Sun, Moon, Stars**	Creation
Square	Signifies Christ is the cornerstone	**Circle**	Life without end
Serpent and fruit	Promise to Adam and Eve (Gn 3)	**Altar**	Prophecy of Malachi (Mal 1)
Ark or Rainbow	Promise to Noah (Gn 6)	**Hand**	(Is 6)
Ram	Promise to Abraham (Gn 12, 15)	**Tablets of Law**	Moses (Dt 5)
Scepter	Promise to Judah (Gn 49)	**Coat of Colors**	Joseph, type of Christ (Gn 37)
Lion	Promise of Judah (Gn 49)	**Star of David**	Prophecy of David (Ps 109)
Cross	Prophecies of Jeremiah (Jer 11)	**Cloud**	Prophecy of Isaiah (Is 45:8)
Broken Chain	Prophecies of Ezekiel (Ez 34, 37)	**Whale**	Jonah, a figure of Christ (Jon 2)

The last seven are linked with the "O" antiphons:

Hour Glass	Prophecy of Daniel "O Sapientia" (Dn 19)
Silhouette of Bethlehem	Prophecy of Micah "O Adonis" (Mich 5)
Shell	John the Baptist "O Radix Jesse" (Is 40)
Lamb of God	John the Baptist "O Clavis David" (Mal 3, Jn 1)
Carpenter's Square	St. Joseph "O Oriens"
Crown of Twelve Stars	Mary, Mother of Christ "O Rex Gentium" (Rv 12)
Chi-Rho	Christ our Savior "O Emmanuel" (Lk 2:1–14)

Other Christian symbols: the Fish, Alpha, Omega, King's crown, Wheat, Grapes, White Dove
Biblical words: Love, Joy, Hope, Peace, Stars

THE JESSE TREE

CHI-RO

AN EVERGREEN TREE IS
BEST, IF POSSIBLE.

THE CHILDREN CAN
HELP DRAW AND CUT
OUT THE SYMBOLS
WHILE LEARNING ABOUT
THEIR MEANING.

THE BASE ITSELF IS A TRIANGLE. A BUCKET IS EASIER
AND MORE PRACTICAL FOR MOST PEOPLE.

NOTES ON PROPS:

CHAPTER 4

MAKING AND USING PUPPETS

Puppets have a long pedigree in the field of entertainment and they do get the message across. From *Punch and Judy* to modern TV shows like *Sesame Street*, children are captivated by the small characters.

And characters are what they are. Puppets very quickly and easily inhabit the role assigned to them, while adding a magic of their own. Whether it is one puppet character reading a story, or a number of them performing, it is a good way to gain children's attention and interest in presenting a story or theme. With a group of twelve-year-olds, we have made puppets and have written and performed the themes. We made and used glove puppets because these were the easiest to make and operate.

You will need some kind of screen for the puppet operators to sit behind. A table turned on its side might be adequate, if the puppeteers are wearing unobtrusive clothing. Puppeteers must remember to hold the puppets high above the table edge so that they can be seen. The readers can use different voices for the various characters, or simply narrate.

The story of Moses in the bulrushes is a suitable storyline for puppets to develop. The characters can be sock or glove puppets. If you choose to use socks as the basis of your puppets, the characterization will be more like Kermit the Frog, with the emphasis on the head and mouth. You lose out on arm movement, but there might be stories in which this is not so important.

TABLE

GLOVE PUPPETS

With the glove puppet, there is the advantage of a more "human" representation, with an emphasis on their body reactions to each other rather than concentrating on the head and mouth.

The diagram for the glove puppet is in the right proportions, but you should check the size of the hand which it has to fit before cutting it out. It is made in a "Y" shape to facilitate operating the puppet. We made the gloves from old sheets or pillowcase material, then "dressed" them as befitted the character.

THIS BASIC GLOVE PATTERN CAN BE ADAPTED FOR SIZE AS NECESSARY.

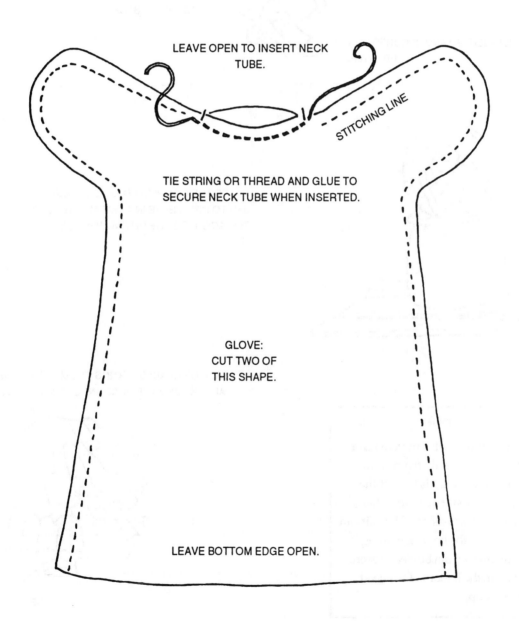

LEAVE OPEN TO INSERT NECK TUBE.

STITCHING LINE

TIE STRING OR THREAD AND GLUE TO SECURE NECK TUBE WHEN INSERTED.

GLOVE:
CUT TWO OF
THIS SHAPE.

LEAVE BOTTOM EDGE OPEN.

THE HEAD

As with the papier-mâché for the sculpted figures (see Chapter 5), you will need newspapers, wallpaper paste, and some empty jam jars. The cardboard for the neck tube can be taken from an empty cereal box.

The head is made from a sheet of newspaper wadded up into a loose ball, the approximate size of a tennis ball. Make a hole with your finger at one end where the neck will be, and insert a cardboard tube large enough to fit your forefinger. Tape on and secure with pasted paper strips.

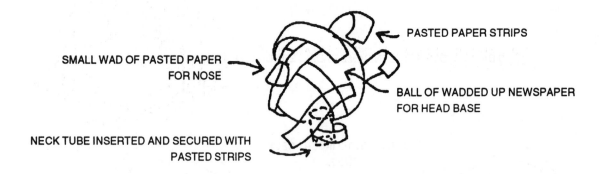

SMALL WAD OF PASTED PAPER FOR NOSE

PASTED PAPER STRIPS

BALL OF WADDED UP NEWSPAPER FOR HEAD BASE

NECK TUBE INSERTED AND SECURED WITH PASTED STRIPS

PLACE THE COMPLETED HEAD ON A JAM JAR TO DRY. LEAVE IN A WARM, DRY PLACE TO FACILITATE THE DRYING PROCESS.

BACK OF HEAD: STARTING FROM CENTER, WORK ALL AROUND THE HEAD, INCLUDING THE SIDES.

HAIR

Hair (for those without veils) can be made most easily from wool, the very thick kind is best. If the character doesn't need long hair, carpet wool is excellent. The hair can be any color, the important thing is that the puppet can be clearly seen. Start from the bottom of the head and work up.

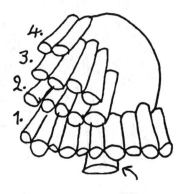

NECK TUBE

TO ATTACH THE HEAD TO THE GLOVE, INSERT THE NECK TUBE INTO THE
NECK OPENING ON THE GLOVE. SPREAD A LINE OF GLUE WHERE THE MATE-
RIAL MEETS THE CARDBOARD TUBE. PULL THE DRAWSTRINGS TO HOLD
THE MATERIAL IN PLACE CLOSELY AGAINST THE TUBE, CHECK THAT IT IS
STICKING AND LEAVE TO DRY.

GLUE MATERIAL TO NECK AND TIGHTEN DRAWSTRINGS.
KNOT OFF AND CUT.

NECK TUBE

> **TIP**
>
> Remember that only the top half of the puppets can be seen, so concentrate on their heads and trunks to give individuality and character. Useful pieces of clothing include cloaks, vests, shoulder/waist sashes, veils, headcloths, turbans, skull-caps, beards, shawls, neckerchiefs, brooches, and earrings, and details such as buttons and pockets.

FINGERS

HAND

THUMB

SOCK PUPPETS

Operating the sock puppets can be done in the same way as the hand puppets—from behind a table. Because they are, in many ways, more intimate characters than the glove puppets, they could also simply sit on their animator's knee and carry on a conversation or dialogue with other puppets or humans from there.

You will need socks of all kinds—plain, striped, etc. (There are often mateless ones lying around!) You will also need wool or fur for hair, red felt or material for mouths and lips, and a variety of bought or made up eyes, including the kind that "swivel" when the head is moved.

Put the sock on your hand to see where the mouth, eyes, and hair all need to go. The mouth moves by moving and bunching your fingers and hand, so roughly the mouth will be at the "toe" of the sock and the eyes on top, made visible when your hand is "bunched." The best way is to try it out and see for yourself.

The movement of the puppets is very important. Your hand, wrist, fingers, and forearm can all be utilized to great effect in both kinds of puppets.

Once again, the best way is to try it and see for yourself—and they are fun to practice with!

These "sock" characters are very good at showing emotion, so they could be used to more advantage in a dialogue situation that is making some "moral" point. They might be used in a play about the disadvantages of stealing, lying, or cheating, or the advantages of being kind, helpful, or making the best out of difficult situations.

NOTES ON PUPPETS:

CHAPTER 5

SCULPTURE AND TABLEAU MAKING

For certain times in the liturgical year, a tableau illustrating an aspect of the event is very effective. A tableau is a group of figures representing or portraying an event: a living picture. In mimed tableau, people "freeze" into the required positions to heighten the dramatic effect of the scene they are representing. In the present context, the tableau is made up of sculpted or modeled figures. A well-known example is the traditional nativity scene at Christmas time, with the baby brought in procession and placed in the crib during the main Christmas service or the children's service, and the kings making their appearance at Epiphany.

Another appropriate time is Lent. On several occasions in school, we have based a Lenten tableau on various Stations of the Cross. (These are scenes showing Jesus' journey to Calvary with his cross, beginning with Pilate washing his hands. They are a traditional feature around the walls of a Roman Catholic Church.) Sometimes we have let these scenes stand in their own right as depicting Christ's journey to Calvary, changing the Station two or three times during the seven-week Lenten period. At other times, we have expanded this theme to incorporate a suitable topical theme. For example, it could be linked to an issue of justice, peace, exploitation, violence, or reconciliation. These areas might help increase the children's awareness (and our own)

of the problems faced by many people in the world today, linking them with the same problems faced by the people of Jesus' time. Another idea might be to link the tableau with something the children are learning in religion classes. Or, it might usefully be linked with our personal journey in the awareness of God's love for us.

The figures we made and used were approximately 2'-3' high, made of chicken wire and papier-mâché. If simply designed and constructed, children of all ages enjoy making them with adult help and supervision.

Although we made male/female figures, none of the puppets represented anyone in particular. This meant they could become interchangeable, which can be interesting if showing Simon of Cyrene helping Jesus with his cross. Which one is Simon, which one is Jesus? Ask the children. Everyone has their own reasons for choosing a particular figure, but interchangability also says something about our lives too. Sometimes we need help, and sometimes we can give help. The figures can be made as specific or nonspecific as desired. We painted ours with a bronze finish, which gave the effect of bronze sculpture. They could also be painted naturalistically or material could be swathed around them to give the more realistic effect of the clothing of the times.

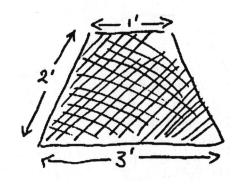

TO MAKE THE FRAME

You will need some pieces of chicken wire, a pair of wire cutters, and some gardening gloves to protect your hands. Follow the steps in the following diagrams, depending on which shapes you decide you want to make. The simplest body shape to make is the cone: Cut and bend a piece of chicken wire into the shape. (Sizes are approximate).

TOP END

BOTTOM END

USE THE LOOSE CLIPPED WIRE ENDS TO FASTEN THE STRUCTURE TOGETHER.

CHECK THAT IT STANDS FIRMLY.

CUT AND BEND A SECOND PIECE OF CHICKEN WIRE INTO A TUBE. DO THIS TWICE.

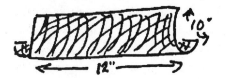

THESE TUBES WILL BE THE ARMS, SO FLATTEN THE ENDS FOR HANDS.

ATTACH THE ARMS TO THE SIDES OF THE CONE STRUCTURE, NEAR THE TOP.

USE LOOSE WIRE ENDS TO ATTACH THE ARMS TO THE BODY.

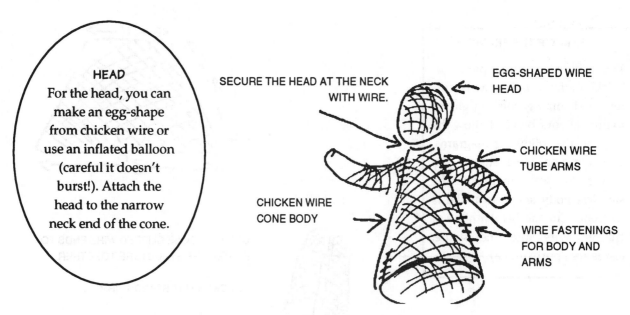

HEAD
For the head, you can make an egg-shape from chicken wire or use an inflated balloon (careful it doesn't burst!). Attach the head to the narrow neck end of the cone.

SECURE THE HEAD AT THE NECK WITH WIRE.

EGG-SHAPED WIRE HEAD

CHICKEN WIRE TUBE ARMS

CHICKEN WIRE CONE BODY

WIRE FASTENINGS FOR BODY AND ARMS

NOW YOU ARE READY TO START THE PAPIER-MÂCHÉ PROCESS.

MORE BODY-SHAPED FRAMES

The cone body shape can be a little uninteresting if used exclusively, so it is good to use different kinds of shapes for the trunk. Rectangles or tubes are also versatile body shapes. Chicken wire tubes can be made longer, stronger, and thicker to make legs. Make sure the feet are large enough and strong enough to support the figure, and that the figure itself is balanced enough to stand alone.

In a Lenten tableau, various figures could carry spears or whips. Veronica would be holding her cloth.

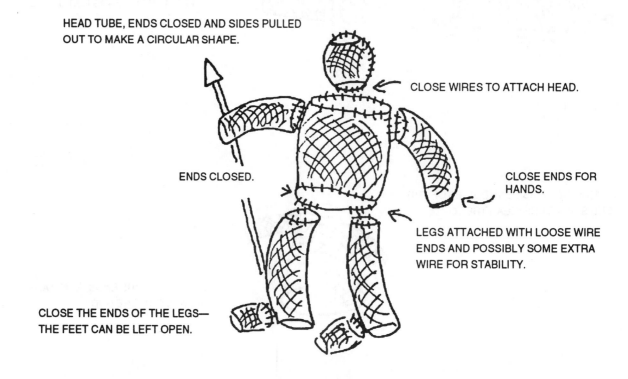

HEAD TUBE, ENDS CLOSED AND SIDES PULLED OUT TO MAKE A CIRCULAR SHAPE.

CLOSE WIRES TO ATTACH HEAD.

ENDS CLOSED.

CLOSE ENDS FOR HANDS.

LEGS ATTACHED WITH LOOSE WIRE ENDS AND POSSIBLY SOME EXTRA WIRE FOR STABILITY.

CLOSE THE ENDS OF THE LEGS— THE FEET CAN BE LEFT OPEN.

TO MAKE PAPIER-MÂCHÉ

You will need:
- lots of newspapers;
- a packet of wallpaper paste;
- a large plastic bowl in which to mix up the paste (mix the paste according to the instructions on the packet);
- some brushes to apply the paste with, or you could use your hands;
- aprons, overalls, or a large unwanted shirt of Dad's to keep some of the paste/water off the children.

STRIPS OF NEWSPAPER, APPROXIMATELY 6" X 12" AND WELL PASTED, ARE WOUND ROUND "MUMMY" FASHION TO BUILD UP THE FIGURE.

HERE IS AN EXAMPLE OF A CONE FIGURE, VERONICA AND HER CLOTH.

VERONICA'S VEIL IS MADE FROM A SINGLE SHEET OF NEWSPAPER, PASTED AND DRAPED.

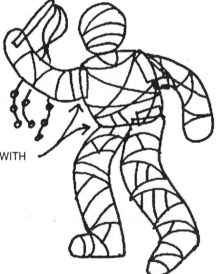

MAKE SURE JOINTS ARE WELL SECURED WITH EXTRA PASTED PATCHES.

LENT SCULPTURE TABLEAU

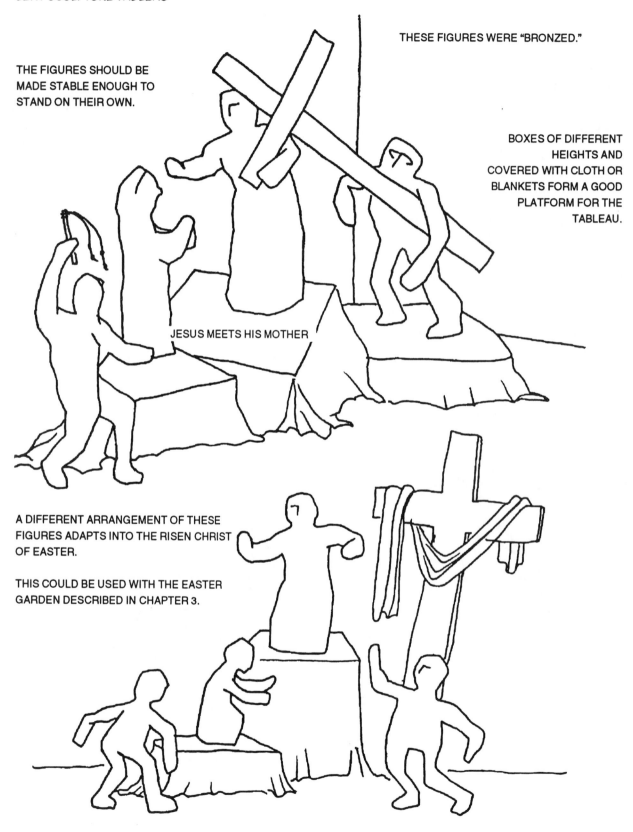

THE FIGURES SHOULD BE
MADE STABLE ENOUGH TO
STAND ON THEIR OWN.

THESE FIGURES WERE "BRONZED."

BOXES OF DIFFERENT
HEIGHTS AND
COVERED WITH CLOTH OR
BLANKETS FORM A GOOD
PLATFORM FOR THE
TABLEAU.

JESUS MEETS HIS MOTHER

A DIFFERENT ARRANGEMENT OF THESE
FIGURES ADAPTS INTO THE RISEN CHRIST
OF EASTER.

THIS COULD BE USED WITH THE EASTER
GARDEN DESCRIBED IN CHAPTER 3.

NOTES ON SCULPTURE AND TABLEAU MAKING:

CHAPTER 6

USING AN OVERHEAD PROJECTOR

The overhead projector can benefit your work of preparing and delivering children's liturgy in a number of ways. It can be used to display hymns and songs with which the congregation is not familiar. Or, the telling of a story may be enhanced by displaying drawings to illustrate the theme—a picture might be revealed bit by bit as the story is told.

Your material may be written, drawn free-hand, or photocopied on to an acetate (the clear cellophane sheets used in the projector). The picture may be black and white or in color. (Be sure that you are not breaking copyright laws!)

Copy the drawing onto acetate and project it onto a large sheet of cloth or paper pinned to a wall. The image can be captured by drawing or painting it on the paper or cloth. The picture could also be projected onto a bare wall or a window.

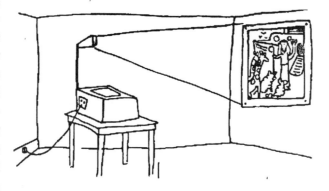

These drawings or paintings can be used for backdrops to a drama or mime. They might be displayed around the walls of the church or hall in the form of a frieze, telling a story in sequence over a number of weeks. For example, the series of appearances Jesus made to various people between his death and his Ascension into heaven, or the series of events from the annunciation to Jesus' birth.

Reproduce a drawing on a window pane by placing sheets of white paper or cloth behind the glass to be painted. Project your picture, which you have first drawn on an acetate, through the glass and onto the sheet. Trace the picture with a fine paintbrush, using poster paints, on the glass.

The paints or markers used should be washable for removing afterwards. Paint in the picture. Children of ten years and over will be able to do this task with adult supervision.

SOME HINTS
• Write in good-sized, legible print.
• Cover only one or two items or points per acetate.
• Use colored markers to highlight words and make pictures cheerful and interesting. Be sure the picture is in clear focus, and be careful not to let any part of your body come between the lens and the screen, especially if you have your back to the screen when using the overhead projector.
• Position the screen close to the main altar, allowing the congregation to see the screen and the celebrant without distraction.
• Switch off the machine when you have finished with an acetate or it becomes a distraction.
• It is not advisable to use the overhead projector every week as it can dull your incentive to use other visual images and become boring for the congregation.

The design of your church or hall might be such that, when you have the overhead projector to one side of the main altar, some of the people sitting at the side may not be able to see. In time, given the space, these people will move to the center of their own accord. If the space is not available for them to move, then it will be important to think again about the value of this medium in these circumstances.

STAINED-GLASS WINDOW

If you don't want to paint directly on the windows, it is possible to make stained-glass windows out of colored cellophane or tissue paper and black paper. These can be pinned to existing window frames, allowing the light to shine through.

Alternatively, they could be attached to a wooden frame with a light placed behind it for illumination.

The design can be abstract or figurative (remember that stylized shapes are easier to work on than naturalistic shapes). Make sure that the design cut out of the black paper, leaves plenty of paper to connect the image and keep it from falling apart.

A

B

1. MEASURE A 2"-3" MARGIN AROUND THE BLACK PAPER.

2. WITH WHITE CHALK, DRAW THE LAYOUT OF THE DESIGN (A).

3. WHEN YOU'RE HAPPY WITH DESIGN, RE-DRAW IT CAREFULLY, REMEMBERING TO LEAVE THE BLACK PAPER OUTLINE INTACT TO HOLD THE PICTURE TOGETHER.

4. CUT AWAY PARTS TO BE FILLED WITH COLOR, USING A CRAFT KNIFE. IT WILL LOOK A BIT LIKE A STENCIL (B).

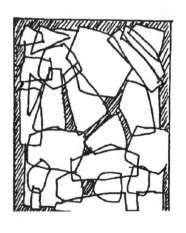

C

D

5. REVERSE BLACK PAPER FRAMEWORK (WHICH IS THE "LEADING" OF YOUR PICTURE) AND STICK COLORED CELLOPHANE OR TISSUE ON THE BACK (C).

6. WHEN THE GLUE IS THOROUGHLY DRIED, PIN TO A WINDOW.

7. IF THE WINDOW IS LARGE, SEVERAL PICTURES TELLING A STORY, SUCH AS "CREATION/GENESIS," OR MAKING AN ABSTRACT DESIGN, COULD BE ARRANGED ON ONE WINDOW (D).

STAINED-GLASS WINDOW ILLUMINATION FRAME

A TWO, THREE, OR FOUR-SIDED LIGHT WOODEN FRAME OF THE SIZE YOU REQUIRE
CAN BE MADE SIMPLY FROM CHEAP WOOD.

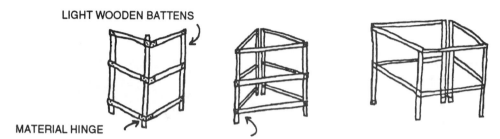

LIGHT WOODEN BATTENS

MATERIAL HINGE

IT WORKS BEST TO TACK ON THE MATERIAL HINGES INSIDE THE FRAME.

THE STAINED-GLASS DESIGNS ARE STUCK OR PINNED TO THE FRAMEWORK, AND A SHADED LIGHT BULB (TO DIFFUSE THE LIGHT), OF APPROPRIATE LOW WATTAGE, IS PLACED INSIDE. (MAKE SURE THE LIGHT IS NOT TOO CLOSE TO THE PAPER OR CELLOPHANE AT ANY POINT.)

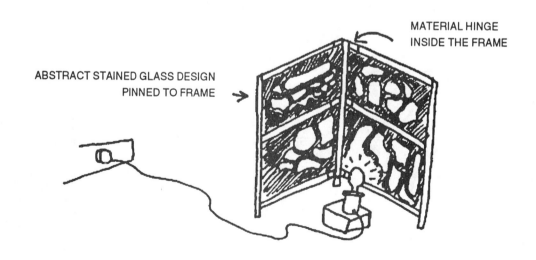

MATERIAL HINGE
INSIDE THE FRAME

ABSTRACT STAINED GLASS DESIGN
PINNED TO FRAME →

DIFFUSED BULB OF LOW WATTAGE PLACED SAFELY
INSIDE THE FRAME

NOTES ON USING AN OVERHEAD PROJECTOR:

CHAPTER 7

MAKING AND USING COLLAGE

Collage is a technique of picture-making by applying paper, magazine cuttings, cloth, feathers, paint, and other non-perishable materials to a sheet of paper, poster board, or canvas. It is a very good technique to use in children's liturgy because the children can contribute materials to the picture and know that they have participated.

Collage pictures can be figurative, where the core of the picture is drawn or painted on a large sheet and other materials are stuck on by the children to complete the scene. For example, you could paint sky, mountains, and some earth-colored foreground, and then allow the children to stick on houses, people, sheep, trees, and birds.

For themes such as challenge, justice, peace, and reconciliation, the children can bring in items—cuttings from magazines and newspapers, drawings, words written on paper shapes, postcards, photographs, etc.—which they feel are relevant to the topic. They can stick them on a large sheet of paper or poster board hung up for this purpose.

Footprints, or paving stones cut from poster board, may be used to make a collage directly on to a wall or floor depicting a journey or way to travel, for example, the way of the cross at Easter. For themes encouraging us to follow Jesus' footsteps and to depict journeys, such as the flight of the Israelites out of Egypt or the journey into the promised land, the collage can be built up over a number of weeks (see diagram opposite).

A PRAYER COLLAGE

Give the children plain or shaped pieces of poster board—butterflies, flowers, hands, hearts, etc. Ask them to make up a prayer and write it on the card, if necessary with the help of an adult. Color the cards and stick the completed cards on a sheet of paper at random or in a pattern. Make a prayer garden or a prayer tree, depending on which shapes you decide to use. They could also be pinned or taped directly to a wall or screen. Once you begin thinking about it, you will have lots of your own ideas.

Ask the children to bring in photographs of themselves which they don't mind parting with. Cut out the faces from the photographs and, when making a collage with children in it, use the faces of children in your class for the children in the collage. This idea can be used when making a collage of Jesus gathering the children around him. It has a magic effect on the children because it makes it so personal for them.

LITURGY BOARD

Collage can also be used to make a "liturgy board." The purpose of a liturgy board is to focus on a theme, especially the more abstract ideas, and help to reinforce the message, not only for the children who can contribute to its making, but also for adults in the congregation.

 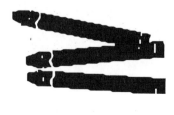 

COLLAGE

BACKGROUND PAINTED ON

FIGURES AND PRINTING CUT FROM PAPER, MAGAZINE PICTURES, ETC.

CHILDREN AND ADULTS CONTRIBUTE "LIVE" FOOTPRINTS FOR THIS ANALOGY OF OUR LIFE'S JOURNEY WITH THE ISRAELITES' JOURNEY INTO THE PROMISED LAND.

LITURGY BOARD

COLORED SHEETS MAKE UP THE BACKGROUND. THE CROSS IS PUT TOGETHER IN A CONTRASTING COLOR (IN THIS CASE YELLOW), AND THE LETTERING IS BLACK ON WHITE. CHOOSE YOUR OWN COLORS. THE COLORS OF THE LITURGICAL SEASON COULD BE A GUIDE.

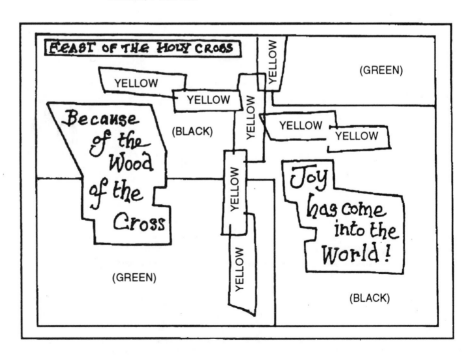

40

NOTES ON MAKING AND USING COLLAGE:

CHAPTER 8

MAKING AND USING BANNERS

Banners make very good "focusing" points, especially if eye-catching, by carrying the theme out to the congregation, or helping to consolidate what the congregation has just heard or seen.

They can be made simply, cheaply, and quickly using a paper collage method. More enduring banners can be made in fabrics. A good way is to make banners for the liturgical seasons—Advent, Christmas, Lent, Easter, Pentecost, etc.—in fabric, and others of a more topical nature from collaged paper and poster board throughout the year.

If you are making a banner for a particular space, for example, in front of the lectern, you will need to measure the space first.

COLLAGED BANNERS

If you have a local printing shop, it could be a good source of large colored sheets of poster board, at not too great a cost, which are a more substantial backing than paper. You could also use it to make up a card and paper template to see what a particular design would look like before making it up in fabrics.

You will need sheets of colored and white poster board approximately 20" x 25", a roll of wide tape, scissors, a pencil, a thick black or colored felt pen, a ruler, tape measure, and glue.

FABRIC BANNERS

All the ideas suggested for the collage banners can be adapted to make fabric banners if desired. It is best to look around fabric shops for remnants that would be suitable to make up into banners, as felt is now very expensive.

The simplest method to make a banner from fabric is appliqué, which is the fabric equivalent of collage. Again, keep shapes and lettering simple, colorful, and clear. A heavier, plain fabric is more suitable for the back-cloth. Almost anything can be appliquéd to this.

There are several books available on making liturgical banners, most of them rather specialized. A combination of your own ideas and sewing skills, plus some of their basic suggestions, could be helpful to you.

Remember that you might have to weight the bottom, and hang them from something rigid like a dowel.

FOR A SIMPLE WALL BANNER

1. Place two sheets of the same color poster board end to end and join with tape.

2. Lightly rule a margin, approximately 2" in from the edge, all around the card.

3. Choose a simple, effective few words to fit in with the particular theme

4. The simplest way is to write them boldly using a black felt pen on white or a contrasting color poster board, for example, "Come Holy Spirit" or "Come Spirit of Life" for Pentecost. Remember to write large enough.

5. Cut around the words rather than each individual letter, which in itself makes an interesting design shape against the backing sheet. Sometimes it is effective to cut out the individual letters (see diagrams).

6. Spend a bit of time arranging the letters and words in a lively, eye-catching design, sticking with tape and hanging up if necessary to see how it looks before the final gluing.

7. You could also include a simple, appropriate motif behind the lettering.

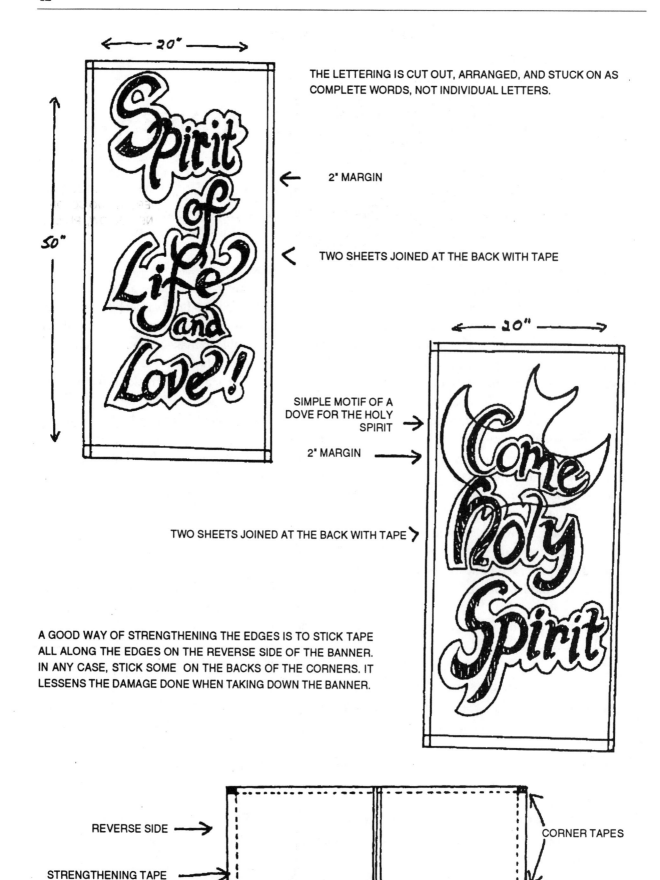

THE LETTERING IS CUT OUT, ARRANGED, AND STUCK ON AS COMPLETE WORDS, NOT INDIVIDUAL LETTERS.

2" MARGIN

TWO SHEETS JOINED AT THE BACK WITH TAPE

SIMPLE MOTIF OF A DOVE FOR THE HOLY SPIRIT

2" MARGIN

TWO SHEETS JOINED AT THE BACK WITH TAPE

A GOOD WAY OF STRENGTHENING THE EDGES IS TO STICK TAPE ALL ALONG THE EDGES ON THE REVERSE SIDE OF THE BANNER. IN ANY CASE, STICK SOME ON THE BACKS OF THE CORNERS. IT LESSENS THE DAMAGE DONE WHEN TAKING DOWN THE BANNER.

REVERSE SIDE

STRENGTHENING TAPE

CORNER TAPES

EASTER COLLAGE BANNERS.

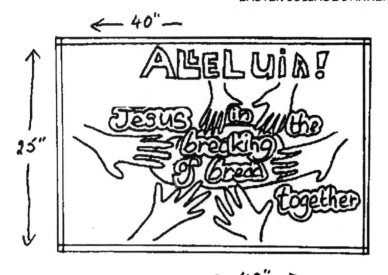

← 40" →

25"

IN THIS BANNER, CHILDREN AND ADULTS DREW AROUND THEIR OWN HANDS IN PENCIL. THESE WERE TRACED OVER IN BLACK FELT PEN, AS WAS THE LETTERING AND BREAD, THEN CUT OUT AND STUCK ON. THE BACK SHEETS WERE IN TWO COLORS, ONE GREEN AND ONE YELLOW, PLACED SIDE BY SIDE.

← 40" →

25"

SEPARATE LETTERS WERE USED FOR "ALLELUIA" AND "CREDO." THE BACKGROUND WAS MAUVE AND IT GAVE A STRONG BACKGROUND COLOR FOR THE SILHOUETTES OF THE BROKEN CROSS AND BUTTERFLIES (AN ANCIENT SYMBOL OF RESURRECTION). THESE WERE ALL CUT FROM WHITE PAPER AND LEFT WHITE AGAINST MAUVE.

THE FAMILY TREE OF CHRISTIAN UNITY IS SOMETHING CHILDREN LOVE CONTRIBUTING TO BY STICKING ON BRANCHES (BUILT UP FROM STRIPS OF WHITE PAPER) OR BY MAKING BIRDS TO SIT ON THE BRANCHES. NAMES OF VARIOUS CHURCHES OR DENOMINATIONS COULD BE WRITTEN ON THE VARIOUS BRANCHES. THIS ONE WAS MADE ON A BACKGROUND OF TWO DIFFERENT COLORED SHEETS OF POSTER BOARD.

YOU CAN MAKE A LARGER BANNER BY USING FOUR OR SIX SHEETS INSTEAD OF TWO. YOU COULD ALSO USE DIFFERENT COLORED BACKING SHEETS.

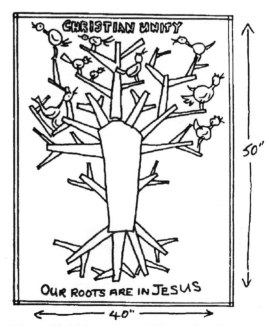

50"

← 40" →

NOTES ON MAKING AND USING BANNERS:

CHAPTER 9

WORKING WITH HYMNS AND SONGS

Singing is a very important part of any celebration. In some Christian traditions, hymn singing plays a well-established part in the service, and in others, the congregation has to be coaxed to sing. In the case of the latter, there is no hope at all of getting them to sing unless the tunes are familiar and the words are provided for them.

Since we are concerned in this book with visual aids, let us look at some of the ways you can provide your congregation with the words of the hymns/ songs.

Start with a small selection of familiar hymns to cover the sequence or format of the service: entrance, offertory, communion, recessional, as in the Roman Catholic and Anglican liturgies.

Type these on two sides of a sheet of paper, photocopy the required number and slide them into clear plastic covers to be handed out to the people before the service, and collected afterwards. (NOTE: Permission must be obtained from the music publishers to copy their hymns. Otherwise, you will be violating copyright laws.)

Number the hymns/songs for easy access.

Sing the same hymns/songs week after week, dropping one and adding a new one every eight to ten weeks. This gives the congregation time to become familiar with the hymns/songs in the church context. Where services are held a number of times weekly in the school context, the hymns/songs may be changed more frequently.

Another idea is to buy a supply of ring folders and add new pages to them as required, thereby building up a collection of hymns/songs.

You may decide to use one of the many hymn books on the market. In this case you will be restricted to the hymns in that book.

Type or hand write the hymns/songs on sheets of acetate and, with the overhead projector, reproduce the words on a screen (see the chapter on overhead projectors).

It is not advisable to print the words of hymns/songs on a flip chart and stand it in front of the congregation as only the few in front will be able to read it. This method will only work for small groups of twenty to thirty people.

Many hymns/songs are suitable to be sung with actions and the children love this. The Lord's Prayer sung by the children with hand actions helps them to concentrate on the content of the prayer. The children could be invited to stand around the altar with the celebrant to sing the Lord's Prayer.

If your congregation is shy about singing out, plant a few singers among the people throughout the church and let them lead the singing. This sometimes helps.

46

NOTES ON WORKING WITH HYMNS AND SONGS:

CHAPTER 10

BRINGING THE MESSAGE HOME

It is essential to help children and their parents to see the word of God received at the Sunday liturgy as an integral part of their lives for that week, not just an isolated event.

In children's liturgies there are many ways of bringing home the message. A drawing relevant to the theme may be photocopied and handed out at the end of the service for the children to bring home, color, and bring back the following week to be displayed on the walls of the church or hall. For themes such as Jesus gathering the children, they could draw and paint a self-portrait which would be hung on the wall surrounding a picture of Jesus.

Completed pictures can also be mounted and hung at home or given as presents to parents.

A simple mounting method is to cut a piece of colored poster board about three or four inches larger than the picture to be mounted. Paste the picture onto the center of the poster board. Cut a piece of clear cellophane two inches larger than the poster board and place it on the right side of the picture, cut away excess at corners and fold under at sides. Tape a loop of thread to the back of the picture for hanging (see diagram on the next page).

If the children are old enough to draw their own pictures, let them do so, bearing in mind the visual effectiveness of strong, simple outlines and bright rather than subdued color.

Smaller children might prefer to color a ready-made drawing, which could be drawn by an adult or older child and photocopied. Mounting on colored poster board or paper also helps to give a strong visual impact.

Many themes are suitably linked from week to week. To give the children a sense of the story of Jesus unfolding, it is good to refer back to the previous week and use some of the same visual materials, adding to them as appropriate. If the series of events leading up to Christmas or Easter were painted on large sheets of poster board or stiff paper, they could be taped together week by week to make a large picture book or frieze for the wall.

Another way of getting children to think of the themes at home is to ask them to bring in the materials you will need in the coming weeks. Explain to them what the materials will be used for: empty cereal boxes to make a cross or to cut hand and foot shapes for themes such as "helping your neighbor" or "walking in the path of the Lord." Excess boxes may be flattened and stored for future use.

Under adult supervision, children might bring in colored beads, buttons, or pebbles for every good deed they did during the week. These may be included in the gifts for the offertory procession.

When the children are dressing up for a mime or drama, tell them the storyline a week in advance and ask them to practice their part. Ask them to imagine they are living in the days of Jesus. They will bombard their parents and teachers with questions as they spend the week choosing their garments and getting into the part. This in turn may stimulate the parents to look up answers to the children's questions and thus get involved themselves.

Coming up to Christmas, appoint a Sunday on which each child will bring in a toy which he/she no longer uses and is willing to give to the poor. When they willingly part with a toy, valuable discussion can be held on such topics as generosity, dignity, self-sacrifice, and feelings.

Once a year, it is a good idea to have a party for the children and their parents. This is an opportunity to display the art work of the past year, get feedback from the children and their parents, and collect some new ideas. This is also a valuable time to invite new people to join your liturgy group.

MOUNTING YOUR PICTURES

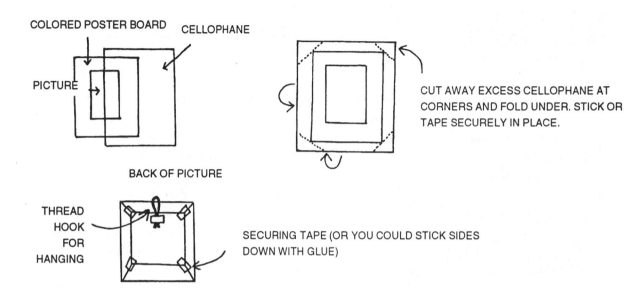

COLORED POSTER BOARD   CELLOPHANE

PICTURE

BACK OF PICTURE

CUT AWAY EXCESS CELLOPHANE AT CORNERS AND FOLD UNDER. STICK OR TAPE SECURELY IN PLACE.

THREAD HOOK FOR HANGING

SECURING TAPE (OR YOU COULD STICK SIDES DOWN WITH GLUE)

FRIEZE ON THE WALLS OF THE CHURCH

FRIEZE OF JESUS' BAPTISM

THE DRAWINGS ARE DONE BY CHILDREN OR ADULTS AND COLORED BY THE CHILDREN.

JOHN BAPTIZING IN THE JORDAN

JOHN BAPTIZES JESUS

GOD'S VOICE IS HEARD AT JESUS' BAPTISM

COLORED POSTER BOARD FOR MOUNTING

THE CHRISTMAS STORY PICTURE BOOK

ANNUNCIATION,   VISITATION,   JOSEPH'S DREAM,

JOURNEY TO BETHLEHEM,   NO ROOM,   BIRTH,

...AND SO ON WITH SHEPHERDS, KINGS, FLIGHT INTO EGYPT, ETC.

FOR A PERSONAL BOOK, THESE PICTURES COULD BE MOUNTED AND PUT TOGETHER AS FOLLOWS:

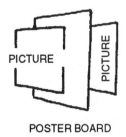

POSTER BOARD

PUT ONE PICTURE ON EACH SIDE OF A PIECE OF POSTER BOARD. PUT THE PIECES OF POSTER BOARD IN THE ORDER YOU REQUIRE AND THEN PUNCH EACH OF THEM ON THE LEFT-HAND SIDE. TIE THEM TOGETHER WITH A RIBBON.

THIS COULD BE DONE ON AN ONGOING BASIS THROUGHOUT THE LITURGICAL YEAR, SO THAT THE CHILDREN WOULD EVENTUALLY HAVE A PICTURE BOOK OF THE LIFE OF JESUS. FOR OLDER CHILDREN, THE APPROPRIATE SCRIPTURE REFERENCES COULD BE INCLUDED.

MODEL DESERT OR EASTER GARDEN

For the weeks covering the story of John the Baptist and Jesus' baptism, the children might like to make a miniature desert.

Start by filling a tray with sand. Add a cluster of stones for boulders. Sink a mirror in the sand to serve as a pond at an oasis. John might sleep in the shade under the boulders or he might have a tent. Make a tent frame with lollipop sticks, clay, and cloth. The following week, to denote a new season, add some flowers to the desert and maybe a tent or two extra. Put up a sign with a lollipop stick and white poster board. If you are very adventurous, make some people from pipe cleaners and colored cloth or from clay. Camels may be added if the children have them in their play boxes.

MAKING PIPE-CLEANER PEOPLE

The size of the pipe-cleaner people depends on the size of your model. These are two basic figures made with either two or three pipe cleaners. The smaller one stands at 3" high, the taller one at just over 5" high. Stand them in a piece of playdough or plasticine and "dress" in scraps of colored paper or tissue paper. The foil wrappings from candy are a useful source of gold, silver, and colored decoration or "jewelry."

MATERIALS FOR EASTER GARDEN:

- one tea tray;
- builders sand or sea sand;
- lollipop sticks;
- a small piece of broken mirror.
- tiny dried or artificial flowers;

- some stones as big as an adult fist, and some smaller;
- white poster board;
- clay;
- small pieces of brown, blue, or white cloth;

FIGURE MADE FROM 2 PIPE CLEANERS

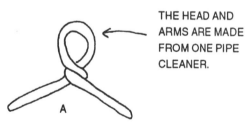

THE HEAD AND ARMS ARE MADE FROM ONE PIPE CLEANER.

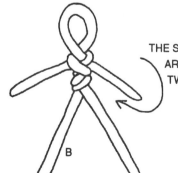

THE SECOND PIPE CLEANER IS BENT AROUND THE NECK, GIVEN A FEW TWISTS FOR THE BODY, AND THE REST IS LEFT AS THE LEGS.

FIGURE MADE FROM 3 PIPE CLEANERS

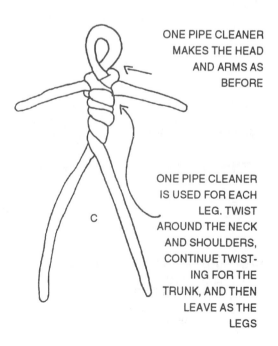

ONE PIPE CLEANER MAKES THE HEAD AND ARMS AS BEFORE

ONE PIPE CLEANER IS USED FOR EACH LEG. TWIST AROUND THE NECK AND SHOULDERS, CONTINUE TWISTING FOR THE TRUNK, AND THEN LEAVE AS THE LEGS

DRESSING THE PIPE CLEANER PEOPLE

CIRCLE STUCK ON AS FACE

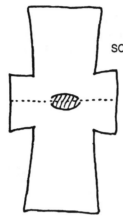

SCRAPS OF COLORED PAPER OR TISSUE PAPER, CUT INTO SIMPLE SHAPES, OR FOLDED AROUND THE FIGURE, MAKE COLORFUL COSTUMES.

IF THE FIGURES ARE DRESSED WHILE STRAIGHT, THEY CAN BE BENT INTO SHAPE AFTERWARDS.

CLAY BASE

MAKING CLAY PEOPLE

THINLY ROLLED SQUARE OF CLAY WILL MAKE HAIR OR HEAD COVERING.

 Head

INDENT TWO EYES IN A BALL OF CLAY.

VARIOUS BODY SHAPES BASED ON THE CONE OR CYLINDER CAN BE MADE.

ARMS AND LEGS ARE MADE FROM ROLLED-OUT LENGTHS OF CLAY, PINCHED INTO PLACE.

YOU CAN USE A BLUNT PEN-CIL, A LOLLIPOP STICK, OR A CLAY SPATULA TO MOLD AND PINCH INTO PLACE.

THEY CAN BE ROLLED AS INDIVIDUAL ARMS AND LEGS OR AS ONE CONTINUOUS LENGTH.

ANIMALS

ANIMALS WITH LONG LEGS OR NECKS WILL NEED SUPPORT. A PIECE OF WIRE WITH CLAY WRAPPED AROUND IT, A THIN WIRE COAT HANGER, OR A PIPE CLEANER WILL DO.

CAMEL

DONKEY OR HORSE SHAPE

SHEEP, DOG OR SMALL ANIMAL SHAPE

DOTTED LINES INDICATE WIRE INSERTS FOR SUPPORT.

PIECE OF STRING OR WOOL

MINIATURE EASTER GARDEN

A MINIATURE EASTER GARDEN CAN BE MADE IN A SIMILAR WAY.

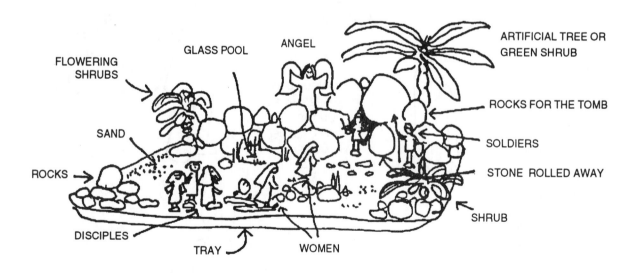

FLOWERING SHRUBS

GLASS POOL

ANGEL

ARTIFICIAL TREE OR GREEN SHRUB

ROCKS FOR THE TOMB

SOLDIERS

STONE ROLLED AWAY

SHRUB

SAND

ROCKS

DISCIPLES

TRAY

WOMEN

THIS KIND OF FORMAT COULD FORM THE BASIS OF YOUR EASTER GARDEN, BE IT LARGE OR SMALL. IT COULD ALSO FORM THE BASIS OF A DESERT WITH AN OASIS BY REMOVING THE SHRUBS AND ADDING TENTS, ETC.

NOTES ON BRINGING THE MESSAGE HOME:

CHAPTER 11

THEMES AND ABSTRACT THEMES

The readings for the Sunday liturgy follow a three-year cycle. We have listed, in Chapter 12, the first two readings and the gospel for each Sunday of the three years of the Roman Lectionary.

We usually pick the theme for the liturgy from the gospel and first reading, which normally link into each other. On occasion we have found that the main theme is not concrete enough to get the message across to the children in the short time available and have picked the theme from the second reading instead.

Often one theme stands out from the readings of the day and sometimes several themes present themselves and you have to choose. In our list of readings we have given you one or two themes for each gospel.

When a preparing children's liturgy, you will need to read the three readings, choose a theme, and then decide on your presentation. In our listings in Chapter 12, we refer you to chapters in this book which we think you might find helpful for each Sunday. The needs of each liturgy group will, of course, be different and our aim is not to swamp you with our ideas, but to help you tap into your own resources.

Some themes are quite abstract and do not lend themselves to mime, puppetry, etc. In these cases, you may be able to use imagery such as in the gospel of the 18th Sunday of Year B, Jn 6:24–35: "I am the bread of life." Ask the children what food is needed for the body. Prepare a collage of a family around a meal table or have some food such as bread, fruit, water, etc., on a table to remind the children of earthly food. Then talk about food for the soul: love, kindness, sensitivity, helpfulness, prayerfulness, praise of God, etc. Prepare a collage using magazine cut-outs or drawings to demonstrate the different types of nourishment for the soul. Talk about how it feels to give and to receive food for the soul.

Another example occurs on the 21st Sunday of Year C, Lk 13:22–30: "Try your best to enter by the narrow door." This one could be dealt with in terms of the different levels of friendship in the child's life: someone they know to see but not to speak to, someone they say "hello!" to, their classmate, neighbor, best friend. Who would they invite to a party or to stay over at their house? Who do they think Jesus would invite to stay over at his house? What must we do to be Jesus' friend?

Give the children circles of poster board and ask them to draw their faces. Stick these around a picture of Jesus who is welcoming them into his house.

Are there people who might choose not to go to Jesus' house?

Keep notes from year to year, especially if the presentation was well received, as you may not remember when the same theme comes up again.

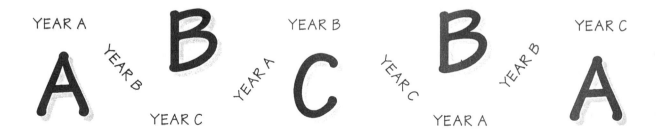

YEAR A   YEAR B   YEAR C
A   YEAR B   B   YEAR A   C   YEAR C   B   YEAR B   A
YEAR C   YEAR A

NOTES ON THEMES AND ABSTRACT THEMES:

THEMES AND APPROACHES
FOR EACH SUNDAY

We took our themes, or ideas to be illustrated, normally from the gospel reading of the day in the Roman Lectionary. In the third column, we refer to the chapters or approaches in this book which we think are most suitable. We have grouped suggestions for all three Sundays of the cycle together. You may, of course, vary these to suit yourself, but remember that you will begin to lose the interest of the people if you use the same approaches too often.

READINGS	THEME	APPROACHES
ADVENT		
1st Sunday		
Year A		
Is 2:1–5	The Son of Man is coming at an	Mime tableau with narrator,
Rom 13:11–14	hour you do not expect.	props, and costumes
Mt 24:37–44		
Year B		
Is 63:16–17, 19, 64:2–7	Stay awake.	Start Christmas storybook
1 Cor 1:3–9		Begin preparing symbols for
Mk 13:33–37		Jesse Tree
Year C		
Jer 33:14–16	Stay awake.	Liturgy board
1 Thes 3:12–4:2		
Lk 21:25–28, 34–36		
2nd Sunday		
Year A		
Is 11:1–10	Repent.	Repent banner
Rom 15:4–9	(John the Baptist)	Mime in costume with narrator
Mt 3:1–12		
Year B		
Is 40:1–5, 9–11	Repent.	Bringing the message home:
2 Pt 3:8–14	(John the Baptist)	model desert
Mk 1:1–8		Liturgy Board
Year C		
Bar 5:1–9	Make a straight path for the	Props: symbols of baptism
Phil 1:4–6, 8–11	Lord.	
Lk 3:1–6		

READINGS	THEME	APPROACHES

3rd Sunday
Year A
    Is 35:1–6,10
    Jas 5:7–10
    Mt 11:2–11
	John the Baptist: Are you the one who is to come?	Drama in costume with props
		Assemble Jesse Tree symbols

Year B
    Is 61:1–2,10–11
    1 Thes 5:16–24
    Jn 1:6–8,19–28
	John baptized with water. Jesus was unknown as yet.	Props: symbols of baptism
		Mime with narrator, or drama

Year C
    Zep 3:14–18
    Phil 4:4–7
    Lk 3:10–18
	What must we do?
	Share.
		Collage about sharing
		Mime with narrator

4th Sunday
Year A
    Is 7:10–14
    Rom 1:1–7
    Mt 1:18–24
	Jesus is born of Mary who was betrothed to Joseph, son of David.	Jesse Tree symbols
		Christmas storybook

Year B
    2 Sm 7:1–5, 8–11, 16
    Rom 16:25–27
    Lk 1:26–38
	Annunciation	Tableau figures of the nativity
		Banners

Year C
    Mi 5:1–4
    Heb 10:5–10
    Lk 1:39–45
	Mary visits Elizabeth.	Drama or mime
		Liturgy board

SEASON OF CHRISTMAS		

Christmas Day: Dawn Mass
    Is 62:11–12
    Ti 3:4–7
    Lk 2:15–20
	Nativity	Nativity drama
		Liturgy board on light

Holy Family:
1st Sunday after Christmas
    Sir 3:2–6, 12–14
    Col 3:12–21
Year A. Mt 2:13–15, 19–23
 	
Year B. Lk 2:22–40
 	
Year C. Lk 2:41–52
	Escape to Egypt and return to Galilee
	Presentation in the Temple
	Jesus is found in the Temple.
		Wall frieze
		Storybook
		Mime or drama with props and costumes

READINGS	THEME	APPROACHES
2nd Sunday after Christmas Sir 24:1–4, 8–12 Eph 1:3–6, 15–18 Jn 1:1–18	The Word was made flesh and lived amongst us.	Abstract themes Overhead projector Liturgy board
Epiphany Is 60:1–6 Eph 3:2–3, 5–6 Mt 2:1–12	Wise men came to pay homage.	Mime or drama Put wise men into nativity scene
1st Sunday of the Year Is 42:1–4, 6–7 Acts 10:34–38 Year A. Mt 3:13–17 Year B. Mk 1:7–11 Year C. Lk 3:15–16, 21–22	Baptism of the Lord	Symbols of baptism
2nd Sunday Year A Is 49:3, 5–6 1 Cor 1:1–3 Jn 1:29–34	He is the chosen one of God.	Banners Abstract themes
Year B 1 Sm 3:3–10, 19 1 Cor 6:13–15, 17–20 Jn 1:35–42	We have found the Messiah.	Drama or mime with props
Year C Is 62:1–5 1 Cor 12:4–11 Jn 2:1–12	Wedding feast at Cana	Drama or mime
3rd Sunday Year A Is 8:23, 9:3 1 Cor 1:10–13, 17 Mt 4:12–23	Jesus leaves Nazareth and chooses apostles. Jesus teaches.	Drama or mime with props and costumes
Year B Jon 3:1–5, 10 1 Cor 7:29–31 Mk 1:14–20	Repent and follow me. Choosing apostles	Banners

READINGS	THEME	APPROACHES
Year C Neh 8:2–4, 5–6, 8–10 1 Cor 12:12–30 Lk 1:1–4, 4:14–21	Jesus fulfills scripture. Jesus reads in Temple.	Liturgy board
4th Sunday **Year A** Zep 2:3, 3:12–13 1 Cor 1:26–31 Mt 5:1–12	The Beatitudes	Simple Collage Banner
Year B Dt 18:15–20 1 Cor 7:32–35 Mk 1:21–28	Jesus orders the unclean spirit out of the man. Teaching in the Synagogue	Drama or mime
Year C Jer 1:4–5, 17–19 1 Cor 12:31, 13:13 Lk 4:21–30	Jesus is not sent to the Jews only. A prophet is not accepted in his own country.	Storytelling Abstract themes: overhead projector
5th Sunday **Year A** Is 58:7–10 1 Cor 2:1–5 Mt 5:13–16	You are the light of the world. Love	Symbols Liturgy board
Year B Jb 7:1–4, 6–7 1 Cor 9:16–19, 22–23 Mk 1:29–39	Jesus heals Simon's mother-in-law and many others.	Mime or drama with costumes
Year C Is 6:1–8 1 Cor 15:1–11 Lk 5:1–11	They filled the boats to the sinking point. They left everything and followed him.	Storytelling Props
6th Sunday **Year A** Sir 15:15–20 1 Cor 2:6–10 Mt 5:17–37	They filled the boats to the sinking point. They left everything and followed him.	Abstract themes: overhead projector
Year B Lv 13:1–2, 44–46 1 Cor 10:31, 11:1 Mk 1:40–45	Jesus cures a leper.	Mime in costume, with narrator

READINGS	THEME	APPROACHES
Year C Jer 17:5–8 1 Cor 15:12, 16–20 Lk 6:17, 20–26	Beatitudes	Collage banners Puppets with narrator

The 7th, 8th and 9th Sundays of the year may occur after Easter depending on when Easter falls.

READINGS	THEME	APPROACHES
7th Sunday **Year A** Lv 19:1–2, 17–18 1 Cor 3:16–23 Mt 5:38–48	Love your enemies.	Storytelling
Year B Is 43:18–19, 21–22, 24–25 2 Cor 1:18–22 Mk 2:1–12	Jesus forgives sins. The cure of the paralytic man let down through the roof	Drama or mime with narrator
Year C 1 Sm 26:2, 7–9, 12–13, 22–23 1 Cor 15:45–49 Lk 6:27–38	Compassion Do not judge. Your reward is in heaven.	Puppets
8th Sunday **Year A** Is 49:14–15 1 Cor 4:1–5 Mt 6:24–34	Do not worry about tomorrow.	Storytelling
Year B Hos 2:16–17, 21–22 2 Cor 3:1–6 Mk 2:18–22	Nobody puts new wine into old wine skins. The bridegroom is with them.	Storytelling Drawings to take home
Year C Sir 27:4–7 1 Cor 15:54–58 Lk 6:39–45	A good man draws what is good from the store of goodness in his heart.	Storytelling
9th Sunday **Year A** Dt 11:18, 26–28 Rom 3:21–25, 28 Mt 7:21–27	The house built on rock or built on sand	Series of drawings in a collage

READINGS	THEME	APPROACHES
Year B Dt 5:12–15 2 Cor 4:6–11 Mk 2:23, 3:6	Disciples eat ears of corn on the Sabbath.	Drama or mime with costumes and props
Year C 1 Kgs 8:41–43 Gal 1:1–2, 6–10 Lk 7:1–10	Healing the centurion's servant	Drama or mime

LENT

1st Sunday

READINGS	THEME	APPROACHES
Year A Gn 2:7–9, 3:1–7 Rom 5:12–19 Mt 4:1–11	Jesus fasts in the wilderness and is tempted.	Start Lent tableau Make model desert and figures
Year B Gn 9:8–15 1 Pt 3:18–22 Mk 1:12–15	Jesus is tempted.	Mime with costumes and props
Year C Dt 26:4–10 Rom 10:8–13 Lk 4:1–13	Temptation in the desert	Liturgy board

2nd Sunday

READINGS	THEME	APPROACHES
Year A Gn 12:1–4 2 Tm 1:8–10 Mt 17:1–9	The Transfiguration	Lent tableau Storytelling
Year B Gn 22:1–2, 9–13, 15–18 Rom 8:31–34 Mk 9:2–10	The Transfiguration	Mime with costumes Drawings to take home
Year C Gn 15:5–12, 17–18 Phil 3:17, 4:1 Lk 9:28–36	The Transfiguration	Liturgy board

READINGS	THEME	APPROACHES

3rd Sunday
Year A
    Ex 17:3–7
    Rom 5:1–2, 5–8
    Jn 4:5–42
	The Samaritan woman at the well.	Mime or drama with costumes and props

Year B
    Ex 20:1–17
    1 Cor 1:22–25
    Jn 2:13–25
	Jesus drives the money changers from the Temple.	Lent tableau

Year C
    Ex 3:1–8, 13–15
    1 Cor 10:1–6, 10–12
    Lk 13:1–9
	The fig tree that bore no fruit
	Unless you repent
	you will perish.
		Drawings

4th Sunday
Year A
    1 Sm 16:1, 6–7, 10–13
    Eph 5:8–14
    Jn 9:1–41
	Jesus heals the blind man.	Bringing the message home
		Storytelling with costumes and props

Year B
    2 Chr 36:14–16, 19–23
    Eph 2:4–10
    Jn 3:14–21
	God sent his son that the world may be saved.	Puppets

Year C
    Jos 5:9–12
    2 Cor 5:17–21
    Lk 15:1–3, 11–32
	The prodigal son	Mime or drama

5th Sunday
Year A
    Ez 37:12–14
    Rom 8:8–11
    Jn 11:1–45
	Jesus raises Lazarus from the dead.	Mime or drama

Year B
    Jer 31:31–34
    Heb 5:7–9
    Jn 12:20–33
	Jesus faces the reality of his death.	Storytelling with props and costumes

Year C
    Is 43:16–21
    Phil 3:8–14
    Jn 8:1–11
	The woman caught in adultery	Mime or drama

READINGS	THEME	APPROACHES
Palm/Passion Sunday Year A Is 50:4–7 Phil 2:6–11 Mt 26:14–27:66	The Passion (We suggest the shortened version from *The Children's Bible,* or some part of it.)	Bringing the message home: Easter storybook Easter Garden
Year B Is 50:4–7 Phil 2:6–11 Mk 14:1–15: 47	The Passion	Mime or drama with props and costumes
Year C Is 50:4–7 Phil 2:6–11 Lk 22:14–23: 56	The Passion	Frieze Tableau Liturgy board
SEASON OF EASTER		
Easter Sunday Acts 10:34, 37–43 Col 3:1–4 Jn 20:1–9	Mary Magdalene discovers Jesus is gone from the Tomb.	Easter Garden Sculpture tableau
2nd Sunday of Easter Year A Acts 2:42–47 1 Pt 1:3–9 Jn 20:19–31	Jesus appears to disciples in upper room. Doubting Thomas	Easter Garden Sculpture tableau
Year B Acts 4:32–35 1 Jn 5:1–6 Jn 20:19–31	Jesus in upper room	Drama or mime with props and costumes
Year C Acts 5:12–16 Rv 1:9–13, 17–19 Jn 20:19–31	Jesus in upper room	Liturgy board
3rd Sunday of Easter Year A Acts 2:14, 22–28 1 Pt 1:17–21 Lk 24:13–35	The road to Emmaus	Storytelling or mime

READINGS	THEME	APPROACHES
Year B Acts 3:13–15, 17–19 1 Jn 2:1–5 Lk 24:35–48	They recognize Jesus at the breaking of bread.	Storytelling or mime with props and costumes
Year C Acts 5:27–32, 40–41 Rv 5:11–14 Jn 21:1–19	Jesus appears to the disciples fishing in the sea of Tiberius.	Liturgy board
4th Sunday of Easter **Year A** Acts 2:14, 36–41 1 Pt 2:20–25 Jn 10:1–10	I am the gate to the sheepfold.	Abstract themes Storytelling Banners
Year B Acts 4:8–12 1 Jn 3:1–2 Jn 10:11–18	I know my own and my own know me.	Collage
Year C Acts 13:14, 43–52 Rv 7:9, 14–17 Jn 10:27–30	I give eternal life to the sheep that belong to me.	Storytelling Collage banners
5th Sunday of Easter **Year A** Acts 6:1–7 1 Pt 2:4–9 Jn 14:1–12	I am the Way, the Truth, and the Life.	Liturgy board Abstract themes
Year B Acts 9:26–31 1 Jn 3:18–24 Jn 15:1–8	I am the vine, you are the branches.	Collage Banners
Year C Acts 14:21–27 Rv 21: 1–5 Jn 13:31–35	Love one another.	Storytelling
6th Sunday of Easter **Year A** Acts 8:5–8, 14–17 1 Pt 3:15–18 Jn 14:15–21	A promise of the coming of the spirit of truth Keep my commandments.	Collage Banners

READINGS	THEME	APPROACHES
Year B Acts 10:25–26 34–35, 44–48 1 Jn 4:7–10 Jn 15:9–17	As the Father has loved me, so I love you.	Storytelling
Year C Acts 15:1–2, 22–29 Rv 21:10–14, 22–23 Jn 14:23–29	The Holy Spirit will teach you everything.	Abstract themes Bringing the message home
7th Sunday of Easter **Year A** Acts 1:12–14 1 Pt 4:13–16 Jn 17:1–11	Father, glorify your Son.	Abstract themes
Year B Acts 1:15–17, 20–26 1 John 4:11–16 Jn 17:11–19	I passed your word on to them and the world hated them. They are not of this world.	Storytelling
Year C Acts 7:55–60 Rv 22:12–14, 16–17, 20 Jn 17:20–26	May they all be one.	Bringing the message home
Pentecost Sunday Acts 2:1–11 1 Cor 12:3–7, 12–13 Jn 20:19–23	The coming of the Holy Spirit	Banners Collage Frieze Drawings to take home Liturgy board
Trinity Sunday **Year A** Ex 34:4–6, 8–9 2 Cor 13:11–13 Jn 3:16–18	God sent his Son that through him the world might be saved.	Storytelling
Year B Dt 4:32–34, 39–40 Rom 8:14–17 Mt 28:16–20	Jesus sent them out to baptize all nations.	Mime or drama Liturgy board
Year C Prv 8:22–31 Rom 5:1–5 Jn 16:12–15	The Spirit will lead you to the complete truth.	Storytelling or dialogue

READINGS	THEME	APPROACHES
10th Sunday of Ordinary Time		
Year A		
Hos 6:3–6	Jesus eats with the tax	Mime or drama
Rom 4:18–25	collectors and sinners.	
Mt 9:9–13		
Year B		
Gn 3:9–15	The question of Satan	Drawings
2 Cor 4:13, 5:1		
Mk 3:20–35		
Year C		
1 Kgs 17:17–24	Jesus restores a young man to	Storytelling with props
Gal 1:11–19	life.	and costumes
Lk 7:11–17		
11th Sunday		
Year A		
Ex 19:2–6	Jesus sends the seventy-two	Mime or drama with props
Rom 5:6–11	disciples out to the harvest.	and costumes
Mt 9:36, 10:8		
Year B		
Ez 17:22–24	The parable of the	Puppets
2 Cor 5:6–10	mustard seed	
Mk 4:26–34		
Year C		
2 Sm 12:7–10, 13	Mary Magdalene anoints	Collage of drawings
Gal 2:16, 19–21	Jesus' feet at Simon's house.	
Lk 7:36, 8:3		
12th Sunday		
Year A		
Jer 20:10–13	Every hair on your	Storytelling or dialogue
Rom 5:12–15	head has been counted.	
Mt 10:26–33		
Year B		
Jb 38:1, 8–11	Who can this be? Even the	Storytelling or dialogue
2 Cor 5:14–17	wind and the sea obey him.	
Mk 4:35–41		
Year C		
Zec 12:10–11	Who do you say I am?	Liturgy board
Gal 3:26–29		
Lk 9:18–24		

READINGS	THEME	APPROACHES
13th Sunday **Year A** 2 Kgs 4:8–11, 14–16 Rom 6:3–4, 8–11 Mt 10:37–42	Anyone who welcomes you welcomes me.	Storytelling. Liturgy board
Year B Wis 1:13–15, 2:23–24 2 Cor 8:7, 9, 13–15 Mk 5:21–43	The cure of Jairus' daughter and the woman with the hemorrhage	Mime or drama with props and costumes
Year C 1 Kgs 19:16, 19–21 Gal 5:1, 13–18 Lk 9:51–62	The Son of Man has nowhere to lay his head.	Mime or drama with props and costumes
14th Sunday **Year A** Zec 9:9–10 Rom 8:9, 11–13 Mt 11:25–30	Come to me all you who labor and are over-burdened.	Storytelling
Year B Ez 2:2–5 2 Cor 12:7–10 Mk 6:1–6	A prophet is only despised in his own country.	Liturgy board
Year C Is 66:10–14 Gal 6:14–18 Lk 10:1–12, 17–20	The Lord sent them out in pairs.	Drama or mime
15th Sunday **Year A** Is 55:10–11 Rom 8:18–23 Mt 13:1–23	A sower went out to sow seed.	Drama or mime with props and costumes
Year B Am 7:12–15 Eph 1:3–14 Mk 6:7–13	Jesus summoned the twelve and sent them out in pairs.	Drama or mime with props and costumes
Year C Dt 30:10–14 Col 1:15–20 Lk 10:25–37	Who is my neighbor?	Collage Banners Abstract themes

READINGS	THEME	APPROACHES
16th Sunday		
Year A		
Wis 12:13, 16–19	The weed in the field of wheat	Mime or drama
Rom 8:26–27		Drawings
Mt 13:24–43		
Year B		
Jer 23:1–6	They were like sheep without a shepherd.	Storytelling with props
Eph 2:13–18		
Mk 6:30–34		
Year C		
Gn 18:1–10	Jesus visits Martha and Mary.	Mime or drama
Col 1:24–28		Liturgy board
Lk 10:38–42		
17th Sunday		
Year A		
1 Kgs 3:5, 7–12	The pearl of great price The kingdom of heaven is like…	Storytelling
Rom 8:28–30		
Mt 13:44–52		
Year B		
2 Kgs 4:42–44	The parable of the loaves and fishes	Mime or drama
Eph 4:1–6		Liturgy board
Jn 6:1–15		
Year C		
Gn 18:20–32	Lord teach us to pray. Knock and the door will be open to you.	Mime or drama
Col 2:12–24		Liturgy board
Lk 11:1–13		
18th Sunday		
Year A		
Is 55:1–3	Parable of the loaves and fishes	Mime with narrator
Rom 8:35, 37–39		Banners
Mt 14:13–21		
Year B		
Ex 16:2–4, 12–15	I am the bread of life.	Storytelling
Eph 4:17, 20–24		Liturgy board
Jn 6:24–35		
Year C		
Eccl 1:2, 2:21–23	Parable of the rich man who built barns to store his grain	Mime with props and costumes
Col 3:1–5, 9–11		Puppets
Lk 12:13–21		

READINGS	THEME	APPROACHES
19th Sunday		
Year A		
1 Kgs 19:9, 11–13	Jesus walks on the water.	Mime or drama with props and costumes
Rom 9:1–5		
Mt 14:22–23		
Year B		
1 Kgs 19:4–8	I am the bread of life.	Banner
Eph 4:30, 5:2		Collage
Jn 6:41–51		
Year C		
Wis 18:6–9	Happy those servants whom the master finds awake when he comes.	Storytelling
Heb 11:1–2, 8–19		Puppets
Lk 12:32–48		
20th Sunday		
Year A		
Is 56:1, 6–7	Woman, you have great faith.	Storytelling
Rom 11:13–15, 29–32		Mime with narrator
Mt 15:21–28		
Year B		
Prv 9:1–6	Jesus claims he is the bread of life.	Abstract themes
Eph 5:15–20		Liturgy board
Jn 6:51–58		
Year C		
Jer 38:4–6, 8–10	I am not here to bring peace, but rather division.	Abstract themes
Heb 12:1–4		Banners
Lk 12:49–53		
21st Sunday		
Year A		
Is 22:15, 19–23	You are Peter and upon this rock I will build my church. Who do people say the son of man is?	Drama or mime with costumes
Rom 11:33–36		Liturgy board
Mt 16:13–20		
Year B		
Jos 24:1–2, 15–18	But there are some of you who do not believe.	Abstract themes
Eph 5:21–32		Storytelling
Jn 6:60–69		
Year C		
Is 66:18–21	Try your best to enter by the narrow door.	Abstract themes
Heb 12:5–7, 11–13		
Lk 13:22–30		

READINGS	THEME	APPROACHES

22nd Sunday
Year A
      Jer 20:7–9
      Rom 12:1–2
      Mt 16:21–27
	Jesus prepares the disciples for what is to come.
	What then will a man gain if he wins the whole world and loses his life?
		Storytelling
		Collage

Year B
      Dt 4:1–2, 6–8
      Jas 1:17–18, 21–22, 27
      Mk 7:1–8, 14–15, 21–23
	Jesus teaches about law and tradition.
	It is the things that come out of a man that make him unclean.
		Storytelling
		Collage

Year C
      Sir 3:17–18, 20, 28–29
      Heb 12:18–19, 22–24
      Lk 14:1, 7–14
	He who exalts himself will be humbled.	Mime
		Puppets

23rd Sunday
Year A
      Ez 33:7–9
      Rom 13:8–10
      Mt 18:15–20
	Where two or three meet in my name I shall be there with them.	Storytelling
		Mime

Year B
      Is 35:4–7
      Jas 2:1–5
      Mk 7:31–37
	Jesus cures the deaf man.	Mime or drama with props and costumes

Year C
      Wis 9:13–18
      Phlm 9–10, 12–17
      Lk 14:25–33
	Give up all your possessions to follow Jesus.	Puppets

24th Sunday
Year A
      Sir 27:30, 28:7
      Rom 14:7–9
      Mt 18:21–35
	Forgive seventy-times seven.	Mime or drama with props and costumes

Year B
      Is 50:4–9
      Jas 2:14–18
      Mk 8:27–35
	Who do people say I am?	Mime
		Drawing
		Collage

Year C
      Ex 32:7–11, 13–14
      1 Tm 1:12–17
      Lk 15:1–32
	They will rejoice in heaven over one repentant sinner.	Storytelling
		Mime
		Liturgy board

READINGS	THEME	APPROACHES
25th Sunday		
Year A		
Is 55:6–9	Hiring workers for the vineyard	Mime with narrator, props, and costumes
Phil 1:20–24, 27		
Mt 20:1–16		
Year B		
Wis 2:12, 17–20	The first shall be last. Welcome little children	Mime or drama Liturgy board
Jas 3:16, 4:3		
Mk 9:30–37		
Year C		
Am 8:4–7	You cannot be the slave of both God and money.	Collage Puppets
1 Tm 2:1–8		
Lk 16:1–13		
26th Sunday		
Year A		
Ez 18:25–28	Which of the two sons did the father's will?	Puppets Storytelling
Phil 2:1–11		
Mt 21:28–32		
Year B		
Nm 11:25–29	If your hand should cause you to sin cut it off.	Storytelling Dialogue
Jas 5:1–6		
Mk 9:38–43, 45, 47–48		
Year C		
Am 6:1, 4–7	Lazarus at the rich man's gate	Mime Puppets
1 Tm 6:11–16		
Lk 16:19–31		
27th Sunday		
Year A		
Is 5:1–7	The tenants rebel against the owner and take over the vineyard.	Drama or mime Puppets
Phil 4:6–9		
Mt 21:33–43		
Year B		
Gn 2:18–24	Marriage and divorce	Abstract themes
Heb 2:9–11		
Mk 10:2–16		
Year C		
Hb 1:2–3, 2:2–4	If you had faith the size of a mustard seed!	Props Drawings Collage Storytelling
2 Tm 1:6–8, 13–14		
Lk 17:5–10		

READINGS	THEME	APPROACHES

28th Sunday
Year A
    Is 25:6–10
    Phil 4:12–14, 19–20
    Mt 22:1–14
	Many are called but few are chosen.
	The wedding feast
		Mime with narrator, props, and costumes

Year B
    Wis 7:7–11
    Heb 4:12–13
    Mk 10:17–30
	What must I do to inherit eternal life?	Mime with narrator

Year C
    2 Kgs 5:14–17
    2 Tm 2:8–13
    Lk 17:11–19
	Jesus cures the ten lepers.	Mime with narrator, props, and costumes

29th Sunday
Year A
    Is 45:1, 4–6
    1 Thes 1:1–5
    Mt 22:15–21
	Give to Caesar what belongs to Caesar and to God what belongs to God.	Storytelling and dialogue

Year B
    Is 53:10–11
    Heb 4:14–16
    Mk 10:35–45
	Anyone who wants to become great among you must be your servant.	Storytelling and dialogue

Year C
    Ex 17:8–13
    2 Tm 3:14–4:2
    Lk 18:1–8
	The widow pesters the judge for justice.	Mime with narrator

30th Sunday
Year A
    Ex 22:20–26
    1 Thes 1:5–10
    Mt 22:34–40
	The first two commandments	Collage
		Liturgy board on love

Year B
    Jer 31:7–9
    Heb 5:1–6
    Mk 10:46–52
	Jesus cures Bartimaeus the blind beggar.	Mime or drama with props and costumes

Year C
    Sir 35:12–14, 16–18
    2 Tm 4:6–8, 16–18
    Lk 18:9–14
	The Pharisee and the tax collector pray in the Temple.	Puppets or mime

READINGS	THEME	APPROACHES
31st Sunday **Year A** 　　Mal 1:14, 2:2, 8–10 　　1 Thes 2:7–9, 13 　　Mt 23:1–12	They do not practice what they preach.	Storytelling Abstract themes
Year B 　　Dt 6:2–6 　　Heb 7:23–28 　　Mk 12:28–34	The first two commandments	Liturgy board Drawings to take home
Year C 　　Wis 11:22, 12:2 　　2 Thes 1:11, 2:2 　　Lk 19:1–10	Zacchaeus	Mime or drama Puppets
32nd Sunday **Year A** 　　Wis 6:12–16 　　1 Thes 4:13–18 　　Mt 25:1–13	Ten bridesmaids took their lamps and went to meet the bridegroom.	Drama or mime with props Collage on generosity
Year B 　　1 Kgs 17:10–16 　　Heb 9:24–28 　　Mk 12:38–44	The widow's mite	Mime with narrator Puppets
Year C 　　2 Mc 7:1–2, 9–14 　　2 Thes 2:16, 3:5 　　Lk 20:27–38	The question of the widow and the seven brothers-in-law	Storytelling Abstract themes
33rd Sunday **Year A** 　　Prv 31:10–13, 19–20, 　　　　30–31 　　1 Thes 5:1–6 　　Mt 25:14–30	The parable of the talents	Collage Mime with props, costumes, and narrator Puppets
Year B 　　Dn 12:1–3 　　Heb 10:11–14, 18 　　Mk 13:24–32	Heaven and earth will pass away but my words will not pass away.	Storytelling Abstract themes
Year C 　　Mal 3:19–20 　　2 Thes 3:7–12 　　Lk 21:5–19	Your endurance will win you your lives.	Liturgy board

READINGS	THEME	APPROACHES
34th Sunday: **The Lord Jesus Christ,** **Universal King**		

Year A
    Ez 34:11–12, 15–17
    1 Cor 15:20–26, 28
    Mt 25:31–46
	I was hungry and you gave me food.	Collage
		Mime or drama with narrator

Year B
    Dn 7: 13–14
    Rv 1:5–8
    Jn 18:33–37
	It is you who say that I am king.	Abstract themes
		Liturgy board

Year C
    2 Sm 5:1–3
    Col 1:12–20
    Lk 23:35–43
	Lord, remember me when you come into your kingdom.	Tableau
		Mime with props and narrator

NOTES ON THEMES AND APPROACHES:

Of Related Interest...

Celebrating Holidays
20 Classroom Activities and Prayer Services
Stacy Schumacher and Jim Fanning
The authors give a decidedly spiritual dimension to traditional secular holidays such as Columbus Day, President's Day, Labor Day, Earth Day, April Fool's and others.
ISBN: 0-89622-611-5, 136 pp, $12.95

Learning by Doing
150 Activities to Enrich Religion Classes for Young Children
Carole MacClennan
A systematic yet simple lesson wheel approach where the topic is reinforced through sensory activities designed to engage the attention of young children.
ISBN: 0-89622-562-3, 136 pp, $14.95

When Jesus Was Young
Carole MacClennan
This book helps children in grades K-5 understand the life and times of Jesus through activities such as grinding wheat for bread and weaving a mat.
ISBN: 0-89622-485-6, 80 pp, $7.95

Fifty Masses with Children
Francesca Kelly
Appealing themes such as Sharing, Trust, Friends are a Gift, and Talents are explored and supported by appropriate original prayers and Scripture readings.
ISBN: 0-89622-541-0, 200 pp, $9.95

Available at religious bookstores or from

P.O. Box 180 • Mystic, CT 06355
1-800-321-0411